Think in Models:

A Structured Approach to Clear Thinking and the Art of Strategic Decision-Making

by Nick Trenton

www.NickTrenton.com

Table of Contents

THINK IN MODELS: A STRUCTURED APPROACH TO CLEAR THINKING AND THE ART OF STRATEGIC DECISION-MAKING ... 3

TABLE OF CONTENTS ... 5

INTRODUCTION ... 7
MENTAL MODELS ARE TOOLS ... 14
IT'S NOT WHAT YOU KNOW, IT'S HOW YOU THINK ... 17

CHAPTER 1. HOW TO BE CLEAR-MINDED ... 27
APPROACH OR DEFEND: TWO FUNDAMENTAL ORIENTATIONS ... 31
DARWIN'S GOLDEN RULE ... 39
THE ARMORED EGO ... 46

CHAPTER 2. HOW TO ACCURATELY SEE REALITY ... 61
DISTINGUISH THE MAP FROM THE TERRITORY ... 63
THE VALUE OF CONDUCTING THOUGHT EXPERIMENTS ... 77
THE PROBLEM OF THE RUNAWAY TROLLEY ... 85
MASTERING SECOND-ORDER THINKING ... 88
PERSPECTIVE IS A TOOL ... 100

CHAPTER 3. HOW TO THINK CRITICALLY AND DETERMINE TRUTH ... 109

THINKING, STEP BY STEP	111
USING THE TOULMIN METHOD	120
USING THE PRINCIPLE OF *CUI BONO*	124
ASSUMPTIONS—DON'T GET TRIPPED UP	128
SMART QUESTIONS TO REFINE YOUR DECISION-MAKING	140

CHAPTER 4. HOW TO THINK ABOUT YOUR THINKING — 147

INTUITION—NOT AS TRUSTWORTHY AS IT SEEMS	148
METACOGNITION—GETTING A HANDLE ON YOUR OWN THOUGHTS	150
WHAT'S REALLY MOTIVATING YOU? UNDERSTANDING LOGOS, PATHOS AND ETHOS	160

CHAPTER 5. HOW TO THINK IN SYSTEMS — 171

PRINCIPLES OF SYSTEMS THINKING	173
SYSTEMS ARE EVERYWHERE	184
QUESTIONS TO ASK TO ACTIVATE A SYSTEM MINDSET	188

CHAPTER 6. HOW TO THINK WITH INDUCTION AND DEDUCTION — 193

INDUCTIVE REASONING	200
DEDUCTIVE REASONING	223

SUMMARY GUIDE — 229

Introduction

Do you remember back in school, when your math teacher always gave you a hard time about "showing your work"? She may have awarded some points for giving the correct answer, but what mattered more was showing her that you knew *why* the correct answer was the right one. Undoubtedly this helped her see whether you'd actually learnt anything—and that you hadn't just copied the answer from your friend.

The dominant educational model today, however, doesn't actually encourage real learning. We present children with a stimulus (sit them down in front of an exam paper), then elicit the desired behavior (produce the right answer) and reinforce this with a reward (high marks, awards, praise or even just the removal of a punishment). The result is a child who knows the answers, and performs perfectly within these fixed parameters.

But so what? You've probably met someone who really excelled in such a grade-school environment, only to arrive at university and completely flunk everything. Everyone can see why this happens: the "rules" have changed, and what used to work doesn't work anymore. New answers are required, but the student doesn't know what they are anymore... and they don't know how to figure them out.

In this book, there are no answers. It's not about adopting the "correct" mental attitude or performing the right behaviors so that you can earn a reward. You won't be told what the right path is—i.e., "what to think." Instead, this book will show you the importance of *learning to think*, rather than merely knowing the answer. It's the old "teach a man to fish" adage—if you know how to generate and use your own cognitive tools, there is no problem that is alien to you, and no challenge that is outside your scope.

What is knowledge?

Isn't it interesting that human beings don't come into the world already possessing the knowledge they need to survive? At the very start of your life, you knew nothing. Your body was small and weak, and your brain was essentially unwired. Your consciousness hadn't really come online yet, and you had yet to even grasp the idea that you were a separate entity at all.

As your sense organs matured and calibrated, you were able to take in the huge amounts of data that allowed you to perceive the world, and orient yourself in it. But almost as soon as you did this, you needed to selectively filter certain things out. You needed to organize and understand the information coming at you from all sides.

Your brain did what it does best: looked for patterns. You noticed and internalized "rules"—for example every time you dropped something, it fell down to the ground rather than upwards. If *you* fell on the floor, it hurt. If you babbled some words, your mother smiled. You noticed not only how the material world was put together, but how other people seemed to move through your shared reality, how you could act and be acted on. Gradually, this knowledge of the world cemented itself in your mind and you began to gain mastery over it.

You learnt to throw and catch balls, to talk, to hold a pen, to sing. You accumulated understanding and skills, and these competencies gave you a feeling of stability and control in the universe you inhabited.

Today, you have all these abilities in your knowledge bank—you *know* how to walk and run, to speak, to write. You can do all these things automatically and without a second thought, even though when you first learnt them it was an immense challenge.

We can think of knowledge as the crystalized product of learning. While thinking and engaging actively with the world is a fluid, dynamic process, knowledge is the stored data that we arrive at using this process. Using what we already know, we can bootstrap our thinking, expanding on our awareness to make further advances.

So far, so good. The real problem is when we mistakenly believe that *knowledge is the same as thinking.* Thinking is elastic and responsive—it's the process in real time of our living intelligence interfacing with the world around us, asking questions, interpreting data and stitching together working theories. Knowledge is what we bank as already "known"—or at least, it's what we will assume we know until better data comes along to prove us wrong.

Neither mode is necessarily better than the other. Without banked experience, it would be impossible to function in the world. But at the same time, we would never learn a thing, never grow in comprehension or evolve in consciousness if we never engaged our more fluid, open-ended thinking mode. The two states of mind work together—we use our lived experience to learn about the world and bank knowledge, which we then rely on to help us ask more questions, and engage further with our world.

In this book, we're concerned not with data and information, but with process. Not with content, but with the various methods we can use to manipulate that content. We are not trying to earn a prize at the end, but rather gain insight into the optimal paths that lead there.

Finally, we are learning not about the world itself, but about ourselves—because the only way to gain mastery and understanding of the world is to first gain mastery and understanding over the personal tools through which we encounter our world.

That's why, although we'll look at several different theories, ideas, and inspiring people, our goal is to become better at *thinking about thinking*, and grab hold of this ability with conscious and purpose-driven intention. With a change in perspective, we can work from the inside out, learning to strengthen our own inbuilt powers of critical thinking, clarity of thought, independence, curiosity, creativity and problem solving.

As a child, your first task was to create a model—of reality itself. Your brain first had to construct the world around you before you could inhabit it; but it continues to perform this function today. The world you live in right now is in large part an expression of your own mind. Your brain's capacity for pattern recognition and meaning-making is a wonderful thing—but that doesn't mean we don't ever make models that are inaccurate, limiting or even harmful.

When you look deeper than content or data and work at the level of mental models, you are essentially rewiring your worldview, and giving yourself the opportunity to create your own experience—consciously. One way to live a better life is to try and figure out what the right answer is. Another way is to look more closely at the question itself, and how you're answering it, and with what tools.

Mental models are tools

Having fixed knowledge is a great thing—as long as the context in which you use it never changes. In other words, you'll pass the exam so long as the questions are always formatted in precisely the same way as you learnt them. The trouble with the world we live in is that it's always changing. It's a big, big place and there's a lot we don't understand.

We are at a disadvantage if we have knowledge *only*, because of its limited and specific use. We can only apply what we know to situations that are exactly like all the ones we've already encountered. In other words, we know what we know, and that's that. When we encounter a new or different situation, our stored knowledge is worthless. We cannot adapt or respond. In fact, we may not even register this new situation because we are so stuck in our ways.

When we learn how to think, however, we are more fluid. We actively engage with novelty and change, and respond to it appropriately. When we are receptive, conscious, intentional and focused on process, we give ourselves the most important gift of all when it comes to learning: the ability to think in a way we have never thought before.

The analogy is often that critical thinking is like owning a toolbox with a wide variety of different life tools, rather than simply approaching every situation with the single implement you have, whether it works or not. Looking deeper, true mastery over your own cognitive powers is like owning a tool-making machine; one that can instantly fashion precisely the right tool for the job… even those jobs you haven't encountered yet and cannot even imagine.

Your brain is a tool-making machine—if you take the time to understand how it works. Mental models shape your lived experience, your sense of identity and purpose, the way you act and conduct yourself, the way you respond to challenge and change, how you make decisions, and the meaning you create for yourself as you navigate life's endless possibilities.

The thing about mental models is that we all use them, all the time, by default. If you can become *conscious* of the models you're actively using, however, you give yourself the chance to upgrade them. When we are not consciously aware of the operation of our mental models, we make unfounded assumptions and forget that we can change, that there are other possibilities.

Stuck in a narrowed awareness, we become attached to our habits and mental loops. In this case, our brain's full potential is not being realized, and we may be working against ourselves without even knowing we're doing it.

Imagine a night sky, filled with thousands of beautiful stars. A mental model is the imaginary constellation we draw by connecting some stars together. These patterns organize and shape our reality—but they do so precisely because they *ignore* a lot of reality! When we become too attached to our models or fail to realize we're using them at all, we are blind to the thousands of other stars right in front of us. Just outside of our models may lie mind-blowing possible solutions, fresh interpretations, growth, and deeper understanding.

We need mental models to help us make sense of our experience. These are like blueprints for thinking; they ensure we don't need to encounter every new situation and start from scratch, like an infant does. We can whip out our model and use it as a guide to quickly make conclusions, predictions and interpretations of what we see around us. However, we also need to remain aware of when our model becomes a limiting crutch rather than a helpful tool.

It's not what you know, it's how you think

The best way to understand the difference between what you know (i.e. what's called crystalized intelligence) and how you think (what's called fluid intelligence) is to use real-world examples. Again, it's not that either approach is more or less correct (remember, we're not looking for absolute answers that are always applicable); rather, it's a question of being as flexible, responsive and conscious as possible in the approach we choose to take depending on the situation.

Picture a situation where two people are at home and the coffee machine breaks. It's a fancy one, with loads of moving parts and complicated buttons. Person A is a barista and has worked with coffee machines of all kinds for years. Person B knows nothing about coffee machines; they're a science student at university.

Person A opens the thing up and has a look, but is stumped—they haven't used a machine quite like this before. When the machines at the café jam up, the staff usually just rinse the grinder out a few times and that works. But it doesn't work this time. They try a few other things that have worked in the past and then... nothing. They have no idea what to do next.

Person B steps in to try and solve the problem. They, too, have no idea what they're looking at, but they know that when in doubt, make a hypothesis and test it. The machine *used* to work, and now doesn't. What changed in between? Then, without knowing the first thing about coffee machines, they set to work unpiecing the information they see in front of them.

They examine the inside of the machine and make inferences about the function of each mechanism, which they then test, and observe the results. The machine spits out hot water only—what does that say about the coffee beans? They try to connect everything they see into a bigger picture, looking for cause and effect relationships, determining how the whole works as a system so they can zoom in on the problem. They even check the power source, knowing it's a possibility that the problem is not even with the coffee machine at all.

In the end, they fix the machine. Person A actually had more concrete knowledge about coffee machines and had probably "fixed" dozens over the years, but their knowledge was next to useless. It was simply not applicable to the new problem at hand. Person B, on the other hand, was not an expert on coffee machines—*but they were an expert at problem solving and learning*. It didn't matter what the details were, as they tackled the entirely novel problem with something better than concrete experience: the ability to think and respond with flexibility, in the moment.

You can imagine, too, that Person B would be better equipped to deal with *any* problem that came their way, whether they had encountered it before or not. The experience that Person A had could even be said to work against them in this case, i.e. "when all you have is a hammer, every problem looks like a nail."

Of course, this is a very simplistic example. The problems, challenges, and novel situations we encounter in life are a lot more sophisticated and abstract than broken coffee machines—but the principle is the same.

Imagine a busy hospital ER ward. There are countless rules, procedures and protocols to follow for every eventuality, and for every patient rushed in through the doors. A newly qualified doctor might know every single one of these procedures by heart; he might know all the special codes, and all the flowcharts and routines to follow.

One day, a patient comes into the ward with a snake bite wound. These can be critical because some snake venom can kill within mere hours if not treated. The newly qualified doctor springs to action—not only does he know the procedure inside out, he also happens to know a lot about local wildlife and that there are three or four dangerous snakes in the area which could be the culprit. He runs through the procedure to the letter, quizzing the patient on what kind of snake bit him, running through an extensive list of questions even as the patient is losing consciousness.

It takes a more senior doctor to step in and take action. This doctor quickly administers an anti-paralytic to stabilize the patient. By the time the newly qualified doctor had finished running through his list of official questions, it would have been too late. In fact, this doctor would have spent time determining the exact species of snake in question only to realize that the hospital didn't even carry any antivenom, so it would have made no difference.

The junior doctor was not truly *thinking*, but merely behaving in rote ways that had worked in the past. By strictly adhering to the rules and regulations, he missed the opportunity to actually engage with the situation unfolding in front of him. Forgetting that the rules and regulations were there as a helpful guide only, he was unable to drop them when they stopped being helpful. He entered the emergency with knowledge alone, but that knowledge just didn't cut it.

The senior doctor, however, never lost sight of the fact that those rules and procedures are simply tools—that may or may not work. This doctor was able to avoid applying a generic approach to the situation and instead adjusted his approach to suit the problem, as it emerged. Because he understood *why* each of the protocols needed to be followed, he understood exactly which ones he could skip over in the name of expediency—and save a life.

The junior doctor knew a lot, and was theoretically "right"—but he wasn't engaged with the situation in a conscious, intentional and active way. He wasn't able to step outside of his own narrow perception and think about his own thinking. Therefore, he could never question it or improve upon it.

As we move through the chapters of this book, we'll look at exactly what characterizes true thinking, and how we can go about cultivating it in ourselves. If we can figure out how to diversify the models and approaches we bring to the table, and if we can become conscious and intentional in the cognitive tools we use, we can start using our brainpower to its fullest potential.

Takeaways

- One of the most common mistakes humans make is that we confuse knowledge with the ability to think. Human beings possess both crystallized and fluid intelligence, i.e. banked knowledge vs. a method or process for learning and engaging with new information. While the

former is useful in certain specific situations, the latter can be employed as a general tool for tackling problems.
- The aim of this book is to help readers think about their thinking or fluid intelligence. The way we think is generally influenced by a conscious or unconscious model in our minds. This model shapes our experience and perception of everything around us. By becoming aware of the model we follow, we can improve it to include more critical thinking, curiosity, clarity of thought, etc.
- We can increase our metacognition (thinking about thinking) by understanding that mental models are tools we can use with conscious intention. They are like blueprints that help us think about different situations and problems in appropriate ways without spending too much time analyzing them from scratch.
- Mental models shape our entire lived experience, so by changing our mental models, we can also change our habits, our attitudes, our

perceptions, and more. Often, we adopt narrow models that are actively harmful for us because of how they distort or exclude reality. Having the right model can give you an altogether new framework for creating meaning and imagining the possibilities in everything life throws at you.
- Metacognition of this kind improves every area of life, helping us to learn, adapt, evolve, and engage with the world in intelligent, dynamic ways. You need not know much about the specifics of the situation (for example, about coffee machines if you're trying to fix one), but if you have a good model for fixing machines in general, you can tackle a wider range of issues.

Chapter 1. How to Be Clear-Minded

In the two examples in the introduction, prior banked knowledge was not only insufficient to solve the problem at hand, it actively impeded the process. This is what psychologists and managers alike have noticed for years, and called "the paradox of expertise."

Though culturally we all admire and respect those individuals who have amassed enormous experience and expertise, the truth is that it's this prior knowledge that gets in the way of solving *novel* problems. Experts with knowledge in one particular area are often *less* capable of solving problems or generating innovative concepts precisely because they've spent more time than anyone doing the same thing, over and over again.

Expertise may actually come with more fixed and rigid thinking, a lack of flexibility and all the errors that come with it. Experts become experts at using very particular and niche models that mean they resort to stereotyped ways of understanding the world. This works perfectly… until the problem falls outside of their mental schemas. Then, because experts additionally have an identity (all right, let's say ego) associated with their expertise, they may not even be able to perceive inefficiencies or mistakes, and succumb to their old bias and tunnel vision, believing all along they're right. After all, they're the authorities!

All of this is to say that none of us is immune to bias, habitual thinking, prejudice, cognitive errors, assumptions and unconscious psychological influences in the way we create and use our mental models. Stubbornly clinging to "expertise" is not the only possible way we can trip ourselves up, however.

In this chapter, we'll look at some fundamental ways that our clear, open-minded and unbiased thinking can be undermined. Whether you call it a mindset, an attitude, an approach, a life philosophy or a mental model, the way that we think about the world can influence the quality of our thoughts, decisions and understanding.

In the same way as a sophisticated computer can't work properly if it's infected with a virus, your clear, rational mind cannot do its best if it's continually under the influence of something or someone controlling it externally. With this in mind, we aim to maintain our focus on inner personal development, and our internal state of being. We begin within, understanding that it's a question of removing obstacles to our own clarity of mind, and *allowing* ourselves to succeed.

What does it really mean to be clear-minded? Clear of *what*, exactly?

Your conscious awareness is like a lens you peer through when looking at reality. This lens is your personal collection of mental models, your ego, your history, your expectations, biases and prejudices, assumptions, and hidden unconscious material. Just like a lens can be dirty, or warp an image, making it bigger or smaller, or filter its color, your mental models can either enhance or distort your perception of reality.

When we become clear-minded, we become aware of the fact that we are using this lens in the first place. Before we can examine the images we see through the lens, we need to ask about the lens we're using—is it full of smudges? Is it serving our purposes as it is right now, or is it time to switch to a different lens?

Human beings are destined to have a specific, subjective experience in life; there is no option to view reality *without* a lens. However, we are at liberty to change and improve the lenses we use. In fact, this is precisely what we do any time we learn something new, and change the way we think.

Approach or defend: two fundamental orientations

Quick, here's a question for you: right now, what is your dominant way of interpreting the information that comes your way (including this question)?

We all like to think that we are *neutral;* that we are objective data-processing machines in an objective universe, and that we are simply taking in information and responding to it. But we don't acknowledge a powerful intermediate step in which we *interpret* what we perceive. This interpretation is total, constant, and may happen without you being in the least aware of it.

Julia Galef's famous TED talk outlined what she saw as two fundamentally different mindsets, or approaches to interpreting incoming data from the world. The first she called a "soldier" mindset. The soldier approaches new information with a handful of beliefs they've already decided on. The aim is to defend and protect those beliefs from new data, if necessary—as though conflicting data were an enemy that needed to be shot down.

We can see this mindset any time we encounter warring factions, be they literal tribes and nations or simply feuding families or groups of people who have decided they are one another's enemies—believers vs. atheists, liberals vs. conservatives, rich vs. poor and so on.

This reminds us of the fixed mindset, when an idea is settled on *before* new information is taken onboard, and new information is filtered according to what we already "know." As an example, consider a person who holds the sexist belief, "Women are bad drivers." One day they encounter a brilliant woman driver. This data point is a threat; the person simply concludes, "Well, they're kind of a masculine sort of woman anyway, they're clearly an exception."

According to Galef, the other approach is the "scout," which is the person who is motivated by a desire to understand, learn and gain insight into the truth. This mindset is more flexible, since it is fundamentally curious and receptive. It's asking a question of the surrounding environment, rather than marching in with a forceful statement. This aligns neatly with the growth mindset we've explored—new information is not seen as a threat, challenge or competition, but something new and interesting to explore.

To continue with our previous example, the presence of an excellent woman driver might alert someone with a "scout" mindset to think again about their own assumptions and conclusions. They might decide, "Maybe this idea I have about women isn't really true after all." More likely, they wouldn't have believed in such a stereotype in the first place.

There are probably more mindsets than these two, and subtle variations of each. You could approach the world and the new information it contains with more or less active agency, more or less curiosity, more or less ego. You could view the world like a scientist, like a gambler, like a prey animal who sees threat everywhere, like a child, like a parent, like a businessman, as though it's a game, as though it's a gift, or as though it's an epic TV series that you're half-heartedly watching unfold as a mere spectator.

Whatever your orientation to reality itself, it's decidedly *not* neutral. We all like to think of ourselves as somehow centered, with our opinions and values being the obvious norm, while everyone *else* has biases, beliefs, preconceptions and so on. But of course, we have them, too.

At the root of either mindset is not rational thought, but emotion. The soldier approach is driven by fear and mistrust of difference and novelty. This is a basic emotional temperament that craves stability and fears the unknown. This is the person who gravitates toward tradition. Testing one's beliefs is seen as weak.

The scout is guided by curiosity—the world feels like a more friendly and interesting place to them, so they don't respond with defensiveness, but interest. This is the person who gravitates toward novelty and innovation. Testing one's beliefs is seen as a strength.

To find out which one you may lean toward, ask yourself how you view changing your mind. Do you think that you've "won" an argument if you haven't budged at all and convinced the other person you're right? Do you think that admitting you were wrong is embarrassing?

When you meet someone with a different opinion than you, do you ask questions and become curious, or do you silently gear up for mental battle, thinking of all the ways you could prove them wrong? How do you see engagement with foreign ideas and the people that hold them? Are conversations a chance to learn, to bond socially, or to prove your superiority?

Many people think that being argumentative makes them intellectually formidable; in fact, the opposite is true.

Imagine two people enter into a heated political discussion. They both see the discussion as an opportunity to prove which "team" is right, and to boast their superior knowledge and force the other to surrender. It's a matter of protecting their mutual egos—their entire identity and self-worth rests on whether they're perceived as right, and therefore superior.

Can you imagine anything less productive, and less likely to lead to learning, understanding and insight for either person?

The first thing to do is acknowledge that being neutral or objective is an illusion: we all have a subjective perspective we're inhabiting, conscious or unconscious. Our culture is set up to reward the soldier mindset, unfortunately. Whether it's in business, politics, academics or science, so many of us go through the motions of learning or asking questions, when in reality we are only seeking to confirm what we already believe to be true.

Though most of us would like to be the scout, we're probably guilty of being the soldier more often than not. After all, isn't it only our ego's desire to belong to the "right" team (i.e. the scout) that makes us believe we're already functioning that way? Maybe you read the above section and thought, "Well, yes, sounds like a good idea—all those other people who are soldiers should clearly be more like me, a natural scout."

Becoming aware of and detaching from our bias is not easy, but it is simple. First, **uncover** why you inhabit this mindset. In fact, just noticing and admitting that you have this mindset in the first place is halfway there. The desire to defend ourselves often comes from an unconscious belief that disagreement is the same as attack, and there can only be one right person, so it had better be you!

Where did you first learn that being wrong was a weakness or flaw? Where did you internalize the idea that the point of mastery and understanding was not for its own sake, but as a way to bolster the ego?

Try to detach your own identity and sense of worth from your beliefs. If you catch yourself in the soldier mindset, remind yourself that there is no "war," metaphorically speaking. Try some of the following affirmations to gently challenge and **remove** this mindset when you notice it crop up:

"It's OK for me and others to change our minds."

"My beliefs are provisional, and I am always open to learning more."

"I have value and worth as a human being, no matter whether I'm right or wrong."

"I learn for the joy of learning."

"I do not have to compete, convince, or prove anything to anyone."

Of course, sometimes your beliefs *are* worth holding on to. Sometimes, it's worthwhile to defend and justify your position, not to prove your superiority to your opponent, but to clarify for *yourself* why you hold the ideas you do.

We can reduce the effect of this mental block by carefully considering our own perspectives as rationally and objectively as possible. If we have to see anything as a threat to defend against, it can't hurt to imagine our own ignorance, bias and irrationality as the real "enemy." Can we transform our soldier mindset into one where we are fully on guard for closed-mindedness in ourselves?

A great way to do this practically is opposite to our usual impulse—instead of finding reasons to support what we already think, can we actively seek out evidence to disprove it? We need to *deliberately* act to loosen the hold of our own ego and to get our minds to accept that being wrong is not the end of the world, and is in fact a prerequisite for anyone who values learning.

Think about how you deal with incoming data that challenges your worldview. Think about your most cherished personal beliefs and assumptions, the ones that are tightly wrapped up with your own identity and sense of self (you know the ones!) and then put yourself in the position of being faced with strong evidence that these are, in fact, not correct, useful or accurate.

What do you do? How do you feel? The automatic, unconscious response is usually to go into soldier mode ("Evidence against my opinion? Well, there isn't any. That's why I have this opinion… it's the *right* one!"). However, if we want to be in scout mode, we have to be more proactive and deliberate, and purposefully work against the knee-jerk impulses of our ego wanting to protect itself. An expert in doing this was Charles Darwin.

Darwin's golden rule

Charles Darwin, the naturalist whose theories on evolution and the development of species had wide-ranging effects on scientific study that persist today, was not a genius. He wasn't especially good at math. He didn't have the quick thinking skills often attributed to geniuses. Charlie Munger once said he thought that if Darwin attended Harvard in 1986, he probably would have graduated around the middle of the pack. Biologist E.O. Wilson estimated that Darwin's IQ would have been around 130 or so—high, but not quite the level (140) where the word "genius" starts getting mentioned.

Darwin was, however, relentless about learning. He devoured information about all the topics he was interested in pursuing. He hoarded facts and was hyper-diligent about taking notes. His ability to hold attention was legendary, and when it came to testing, his work ethic was tireless. Darwin's thinking was purposely slow because he was so fastidiously detail oriented. He believed that to have any authority on any topic one needed to develop deep expertise on it, and expertise doesn't happen overnight (or in a month, or in a year). The point is that Darwin is regarded as one of the ultimate examples of the importance of hard work and diligence in surpassing natural intelligence.

Darwin's method was so all-encompassing that he even gave deep attention to information that countered or challenged his own theories. This approach forms the backbone of his *golden rule* as he expressed it in his autobiography. The very basic guideline of Darwin's golden rule was to be more than just open to contradicting or opposing ideas—indeed, Darwin gave them his fullest attention:

"I had, also, during many years, followed a golden rule, namely, that whenever a published fact, a new observation or thought came across me, which was opposed to my general results, to make a memorandum of it without fail and at once; for I had found by experience that such facts and thoughts were far more apt to escape from memory than favorable ones."

Darwin completely immersed himself in evidence or explanations that went against his findings because he was aware that the human mind is inclined to dispose of those contrary views. If he didn't investigate them as fully as he could, he'd be likely to forget them, and that created mental dishonesty. Darwin knew that his own instinctual thinking could be a hindrance to finding the truth as much as it could help, and he established a way to ensure he wasn't missing out on any information.

Darwin handled all this conflicting information responsibly. He genuinely considered material that might have disproved his assertions, and took pains to fully absorb every single scenario, anomaly and exception to his theories. He didn't filter out information that didn't support his beliefs; he was utterly immune to confirmation bias. More than anything else, Darwin didn't want to be careless in finding the truth—he knew that a half-cocked assertion solely intended to persuade others without much thought was intellectually dishonest. His thorough method required more time and effort on his part, but he was committed.

Of course, the Darwinian Golden Rule calls back to intellectual honesty and the maxim "Strong opinions but held lightly." It assumes intellectual *humility*, as being unattached to any stances or theories and simply following the evidence.

Uniquely, Darwin forces a dialogue of skepticism back to himself, instead of to others in defensiveness. To himself, he would direct questions such as: *What do you know? Are you sure? Why are you sure? How can it be proved? What potential errors could you have made? Where is this conflicting view coming from and why?* As you can imagine, it takes quite a bit of self-discipline to constantly double-check yourself.

Darwin accurately realized that if you hold the belief that everyone *else* is wrong, you're in trouble.

What Darwin seemed to understand is that the biggest threats to our intellectual and cognitive rigor are often unconscious, personal and psychological, and nothing to do with the soundness of our arguments or the quality of our reasoning. In fact, you've probably encountered someone who cloaks their unconscious biases, assumptions and desires in neutral terms precisely to conceal what is really motivating their behavior. I.e. "it's other people who have irrational emotions and beliefs, but *I* only believe in the objective facts."

Try this exercise yourself: think of something you deeply believe to be true—take your time with this, because it may be that your most pervasive belief is actually the one that is almost invisible to you. Now, imagine you are not yourself, but a person who actually believes in precisely the opposite.

Play pretend for a moment, and *genuinely* try to occupy the other person's point of view. Imagine, if you like, that you are in a lively debate with yourself, as this other person. Really try to immerse yourself in this other worldview. What other priorities does that person have? What does the world look like to them? In what ways might they be right? As you debate yourself, don't worry about deciding who is correct. Simply watch what stories and narratives your brain throws up in the dialogue.

Internet activist Eli Pariser noticed how online search algorithms actually encourage our human tendency to grab hold of everything that confirms the beliefs we already hold, while quietly discounting or ignoring information that doesn't align with those beliefs. We set up a so-called "filter-bubble" around ourselves, where we are constantly exposed only to that material that we agree with. We are never challenged, never giving ourselves the opportunity to acknowledge the existence of diversity and difference. In the best case, we become naïve and sheltered; in the worst, we become radicalized with more and more extreme views, unable to imagine life outside our particular bubble.

The results are disastrous: a complete erosion of civic discourse, intellectual isolation, narcissism and self-centeredness, and a lack of everyday empathy, as well as the real distortion that comes with believing that the little world we create for ourselves is *the* world. When two people from mutually exclusive echo chambers encounter one another, the effect can be explosive.

As a general rule, try to avoid filter bubbles in your own online world. Notice where click history, algorithms and personalized search results are shaping your view of "reality" online. Look at websites like *allsides.com* or *hifromtheotherside.com* to deliberately challenge yourself. Consult a different news site from a completely different country and compare their coverage of an event.

Use a search engine other than Google and access it anonymously. You could also try deliberately seeking out material critical of your worldview. Find quality information and genuinely engage with it. Whether you end up revising your old opinion, making a few adjustments or doubling down on your belief doesn't matter—the task is merely to challenge yourself to do due intellectual diligence. If you do these exercises honestly (which is very hard to do!) it won't take long to encounter what is a greater enemy than the people who don't agree with you: your ego.

The armored ego

The first barrier in almost *any* kind of effective thinking comes from the ego's need to protect itself. Sometimes our thinking is erroneous because we don't see all the factors involved in a situation, or we are too hasty to jump to a conclusion. Those are errors in observation or perception. But those reasons pale in comparison to the ego's power to distort your thinking.

Someone who's underperforming at work might feel the need to protect their perceived skills and talent by deflecting responsibility to the boss who's "always had it in for me. And who trained me? Him! It's all his fault one way or another." Someone who trips and falls yet fancies themselves graceful will blame the fact that it rained six days ago, their shoes have no grip, and *who put that rock there anyway!*? Someone who fails to make the school basketball team will grumble that the coach hated them, they weren't used to that particular style of play, and they didn't *really* want to make the team anyway.

This is what it sounds like when the ego steps in to protect itself. There's so much justification and deflecting going on that it's difficult to know what is real and what is not. Clear thinking becomes impossible.

This all stems from the universal truth that nobody likes to be wrong or to fail. It's embarrassing and confirms all of our worst anxieties about ourselves. Instead of accepting being wrong as a teachable moment or lesson, our first instinct is to run from our shame and cower in the corner. This is the same reason we will persist in an argument to the death, even if we know we are 100 percent mistaken. If the ego had a physical manifestation, it would be sizable, sensitive, and heavily armored (to the point of going on the offensive)—essentially a giant porcupine.

When the ego senses danger, it has no interest or time to consider the facts. Instead it seeks to alleviate discomfort in the quickest way possible. And that means you lie to yourself so you can keep the ego safe and sound.

We try to cover up the truth, deflect attention from it, or develop an alternative version that makes the actual truth seem less hurtful. And it's right in that moment that intellectual dishonesty is born. Are any of those convoluted theories likely to withstand any amount of scrutiny? Probably not, but the ego doesn't allow for acknowledgment and analysis of what really happened. It blinds you.

Let's be clear: The ego's justifications aren't lies that you dream up or concoct in advance. You do not *intend* to lie to yourself. You don't even *feel* they're lies. You may not even know you're doing it, as sometimes these defense mechanisms can occur unconsciously. They're not explicitly intellectually dishonest because you *want* to delude yourself. Rather, they're automatic strategies that the constantly neurotic ego puts into action because it's terrified of looking foolish or wrong. Unfortunately, that's the worst zone to be in, as it means *you don't know what you don't know*.

Over time, these ego-driven errors in thinking inform your entire belief system and give you rationalized justifications for almost everything. You never make any sports team because the coaches always hate you, and you keep failing the driving test because your hand-eye coordination is *uniquely special*.

These lies become your entire reality, and you rely on them to get yourself through problematic situations or to dismiss efforts to find the truth. We're not talking about just giving excuses for why you aren't a violin virtuoso; this manner of thinking can drive your decisions, thought process, and evaluations of anything and anyone.

Let's take Fred. Fred was an ardent fan of a pop star his whole life. He grew up listening to their music and formed a lot of his identity around his admiration for him. We're talking an entire bedroom wall filled with posters of this star, and outfits that were replicas of this star's clothes hanging in his closet.

Late in his career this pop star was put on trial for a serious crime. Fred steadfastly stood by his pop star idol, even as lurid details of his case were reported by courtroom reporters to the press. "Nobody I admire this way would ever be guilty of this," Fred said. "It's all just a conspiracy put together by the people who resent him for whatever reason."

The pop star was ultimately found guilty and sentenced to multiple years of prison. Fred had showed up outside the courthouse bearing a sign that protested his star's innocence. Even as compelling evidence was eventually released to the press, Fred maintained that the pop star was absolutely innocent, dismissing all of the victims' claims by protesting that they were "jealous" and "just trying to get the spotlight themselves."

Why would Fred continue to insist, against all reasonable and provable evidence, that his idol was innocent? Because his ego was so wrapped up in his worship of the pop star that it was predisposed to consider him blameless. For him to believe the truth would have meant a devastating blow to almost everything he valued (*I worship a criminal? What does that say about me?*), and the ego wasn't going to let that happen for a minute—even if it meant making him deny what was fairly compelling proof that the star was guilty.

In your pursuit of truth and clear thought, your ego will rear its ugly head like the enraged porcupine. It has set up a series of tactical barriers to keep you from learning something that might upset your belief system, and it is only after you can rein in your ego that you are open to learning. After all, you can't defend yourself and listen at the same time.

Defense mechanisms are the specific ways we protect our ego, pride, and self-esteem. These methods keep us whole when times are tough. The origin of the term comes from Sigmund Freud. You just might recognize these two defense mechanisms put forth by his daughter, Anna Freud: denial and rationalization.

Denial is one of the most classic defense mechanisms because it is easy to use. Suppose you discovered that you were performing poorly at your job. "No," you might say, "I don't believe that report ranking all of the employees. There's no way I can be last. Not in this world. The computer added up the scores incorrectly."

What is true is simply claimed to be false, as if that makes everything go away. You are acting as if a negative fact doesn't exist. Sometimes we don't realize when we do this, especially in situations that are so dire they actually appear fantastical to us.

All you have to do is say "no" often enough and you might begin to believe yourself, and that's where the appeal of denial lies. You are actually changing your reality, where other defense mechanisms merely spin it to be more acceptable. Denial is actually the most dangerous defense mechanism, because even if there is a dire problem, it is ignored and never fixed. If someone continued to persist in the belief they were an excellent driver, despite a string of accidents in the past year, it's unlikely they would ever seek to practice and improve their driving skills.

Rationalization, on the other hand, is when you explain away something negative.

It is the art of making excuses. The bad behavior or fact still remains, but it is turned into something unavoidable because of circumstances out of your control. The bottom line is anything negative is not your fault and you shouldn't be held accountable for it. It's never a besmirching of your abilities. Rationalization is an extremely convenient tactic, limited only by your imagination.

Building on the same prior example of poor job performance, this is easily explained away by the following: your boss secretly hating you, your co-workers plotting against you, the computer being biased against your soft skills, unpredictable traffic affecting your commute, and having two jobs at once. These flimsy excuses are what your ego needs to protect itself.

Rationalization is the embodiment of the *sour grapes fable*: A fox wanted to reach some grapes at the top of a bush, but he couldn't leap high enough. To make himself feel better about his lack of leaping ability, and to comfort himself about his lack of grapes, he told himself the grapes looked sour anyway, so he wasn't missing out on anything. He was still hungry, but he'd rather be hungry than admit his failure.

Rationalization can also help us feel at peace with poor decisions we've made with phrases such as, "It was going to happen at some point anyway." Rationalization ensures you never have to face failure, rejection, or negativity. It's always someone else's fault!

Those are not the only defense mechanisms. You can be sure that as many different lies as there are to tell oneself, there are different ways to tell them. *Projection* is a classic one, and is basically the mental trick we play anytime we first disown an uncomfortable truth and then locate it somewhere else—i.e., we magically find it in other people. The cheater who is suddenly suspicious of their own partner, for example, gets to protect themselves from confronting the horrible truth about who *they* are—by essentially confronting that horrible truth in some imagined other.

A sexually repressed man who is deeply attached to the image of himself as chaste and righteous may see a woman that he personally finds attractive, and immediately judge her for being promiscuous. This judgment tells you more about the unwanted parts of his own psyche than anything about the woman in question. But more importantly, it completely destroys the man's ability to think with clarity and honesty on this topic. As long as his defense mechanisms are working to keep him from comprehending the *whole* truth, his ego will drive his perception of the world. He will see his own bias reflected back at him, and mistake it for reality.

Other defense mechanisms include *displacement* (channelling your emotions toward a more acceptable target, like kicking the dog when you get home from work instead of kicking yourself for staying in a job you hate but don't have the courage to leave); *reaction formation* (behaving in a completely opposite way as though to cancel out the thing you wish wasn't true, like that cocky, arrogant person who is actually deeply insecure about themselves); and *sublimation* (converting undesirable urges and drives into "higher" emotions or activities, such as working through your aggression by taking up rugby... or local politics).

While these tactics are comforting, where do reality and truth go amidst all of this? Out the window, mostly. Intellectual honesty requires you to first defeat your natural tendencies to be dishonest. Thoughts dictated by self-protection don't overlap with clear, objective thoughts.

Psychoanalytics aside, the main point is that all of these mechanisms will sit hidden in the background and quietly distort and influence your rational thinking until you can take them out into the open and look at them objectively. Remember that *defense* mechanisms exist in response to the perception of an *attack*. But there is no need for a defense if there is no attack.

Perhaps the first conscious act of reworking your mental models to your own benefit is to reframe how you experience being wrong, or even receiving criticism. Adopt the scout mindset and deliberately retrain yourself to see counterevidence not as an attack on you, but an invitation to re-appraise the current model, and, best of all, to learn and improve.

When you can derive your sense of identity and worthiness not from holding the right belief (i.e. from content) but from willingness to engage in true learning (i.e. from the process) then being wrong is not uncomfortable, and doesn't trigger the need to flee the truth and shield oneself with defense mechanisms. After all, when we protect ourselves from a painful truth, we are still shielding ourselves from the truth—and nothing could take us further from genuine learning.

Defense mechanisms come with a hefty dose of shame. They only exist because somewhere along the line, we've told ourselves a story about what is and isn't acceptable. What is unacceptable is then unacknowledged.

Instead, commit right now to approaching yourself—*all* of yourself—with compassion, curiosity and a genuine desire to understand and improve. Everybody uses defense mechanisms—this in itself is nothing to be ashamed of, either. Use a little humor, dig your ego out of the equation and remind yourself that you can always derive a far deeper, more satisfying sense of identity from knowing that you are able to tolerate the truth in service of becoming a better person—even if it's a bit uncomfortable sometimes!

Takeaways

- Every single person is susceptible to falling prey to old, outdated thinking habits, biases, cognitive distortions, etc. Experts in particular, for all their knowledge, are notorious for being unable to escape their preconceived notions and rigid thinking because they have become accustomed to applying the same models over and over. To rid ourselves of this issue, we must learn how to be more clear-minded.
- Being clear-minded means seeing reality without the distortion of our bias, expectations, prejudices, assumptions, unconscious drives or cognitive errors. Contrary to what we

think, our orientation to reality is never neutral. The mindset we hold, consciously or unconsciously, influences our perception, and the content and quality of our thoughts.
- There are two fundamental orientations to the unknown: approach or defend. The scout or growth mindset adopts the former strategy and embraces the new with curiosity and humility; the soldier or fixed mindset encounters the unknown intending only to defend already-held beliefs. We can embrace a scout mindset by remembering that being wrong is not a flaw or weakness, but a necessary part of learning.
- Too often, we attempt to confirm and reinforce things we already believe to be true. However, the key to being clear-headed is actually the exact opposite: actively seeking things that go against what we think. Darwin's golden rule is to deliberately entertain information that conflicts with deeply held beliefs, so as to guard against intellectual blind spots.

- The primary factor that prevents us from being open to thoughts, opinions, or facts contrary to our beliefs is our armored ego. An armored ego is a threat to learning and understanding. It is the need we feel to justify away mistakes, erroneous modes of thinking, etc., instead of taking steps to acknowledge these mistakes and improve on them. We need to become aware of unconscious defense mechanisms so we can remove them and see with more clarity.

Chapter 2. How to accurately see reality

The more and more you look at ... well, *the way you look at things*, the more you'll realize just how difficult it really is to make significant shifts. This is because it's something none of us does automatically. Every day you more or less trust the data coming in from your sense organs, you generally believe what you see and hear around you, and you have no reason not to take your own word for it as you tell yourself endless mental stories day after day.

But it takes something extra—some deliberate and purpose-driven decision to be different—to switch us out of habitual, auto-pilot behavior and into conscious and autonomous action.

How do you see the world?

What do you see and what don't you see?

Is what you're perceiving accurate or useful?

How does your mental model influence the way you see?

What effect does this have on your life, and do you like this outcome?

You can never see things from another angle unless you are willing to acknowledge that you are currently viewing things from any angle in the first place. You can never dig deeper if you have entirely convinced yourself that you are already seeing is all there is to see. In essence, our mental models tell us who we are, how the world works, and what is possible for us. Before you take that at face value, isn't it worth examining these mental models?

Being clear-minded was the goal of the previous chapter—i.e., learning to divest ourselves of those obstacles that stand between us and the world we are trying to more properly understand. But simply being free of bias and self-delusion doesn't mean we automatically see reality perfectly. We also need to consider the quality and accuracy of the models we use—i.e., how well they allow us to interact with our world. We need to find out whether our way of looking at reality is justified.

Does it actually work, in other words? We need to go back to the drawing board and remember why we have mental models the first place. The problem is not in using models, but in using them incorrectly. Let's take a closer look at how we can *consciously* use our mental models, rather than being *unconsciously* influenced by them.

Distinguish the map from the territory

"... the teaching is merely a vehicle to describe the truth. Don't mistake it for the truth itself. A finger pointing at the moon is not the moon. The finger is needed to know where to look for the moon, but if you mistake the finger for the moon itself, you will never know the real moon. The teaching is like a raft that carries you to the other

shore. The raft is needed, but the raft is not the other shore. An intelligent person would not carry the raft around on his head after making it across to the other shore. Bhikkhus, my teaching is the raft which can help you cross to the other shore beyond birth and death. Use the raft to cross to the other shore, but don't hang on to it as your property. Do not become caught in the teaching. You must be able to let it go."

— *Thich Nhat Hanh*

The concept that the "map is not the territory" is an old sentiment, one that's been expressed by many in various ways, including by philosophers, entrepreneurs, and Tibetan Buddhists like Thich Nhat Hanh. The idea is simple: the description of a thing, or the symbols we use for it, or any abstraction or model we use to try to understand it, *is not the thing itself.*

Every time you use a psychological model to understand someone's behavior, a mental model to understand your own behavior, or even a scientific or religious framework to understand the world around you, you're using a "map." Maps are necessarily simplified abstractions of much larger, more complex phenomena, and there's nothing wrong with using them. In fact, it's hard to imagine a world where we don't use these intellectual tools to analyze and make sense of our experience.

The trouble is not in using a map, but in forgetting that it's just that—a picture of reality and not reality itself. The world out there (and, to be fair, *in* here) can be a frighteningly complicated thing, and you could be forgiven for coming to rely too heavily on maps, even ones that don't work particularly well.

Maps are representations of the world, but they are not the world. Furthermore, a map is only "correct" as far as it is useful in allowing us to explain and interpret what we see in reality. The danger is in holding the image as more significant than the thing it's meant to portray. Here's an example:

"All software engineers are nerdy guys."

"Well, I'm a software engineer and I'm not a nerd. Plus, I'm a woman!"

"Sure, I guess, but then you're not a *real* software engineer..."

When we cling to a map of how the world is (for example, the belief that all software engineers are nerdy guys) but find it actually doesn't represent reality all that well (for example, discovering a non-nerdy female one), we should rightly adapt the model or else throw it away entirely. Unfortunately, many of us choose to stick with the map despite the evidence and try to reinterpret reality so that it fits the map better (for example, claiming that your belief is still correct and the female non-nerdy software engineer is a fluke or outlier, or not even a software engineer at all).

Sometimes these maps can be useful general rules of thumb. The psychologist Dan Ariely has talked about how we do not have the cognitive power to analyze and conceptualize everything from scratch, and so we use general rules to help reduce the load on our brains. So when we come across a software engineer, we assume they are nerdy guys because that has been our general observation, making it likely that our assumption is true. However, remembering that the map is not the territory is a smart way to keep cognizant of the fact that you are using mental models in the first place, and that these models can and should adapt or be used according to where they fit the best. We can take something to be generally true without assuming that it is always so. That way, we keep an open mind while retaining the benefits of these rules of thumb.

One obvious problem could be that your map is wrong. The entire premise of cognitive behavior therapy, for example, is that the cognitive "maps" you use are no longer accurately reflecting reality and need an update. When you remind yourself that the thoughts you have about reality are not *the same as* reality, you put yourself in the supremely empowered position of being able to change them. You can then work on devising maps that are more accurate or choose ones that are more useful in getting you the results you want.

Maps are not just on the individual scale, of course. Over the millennia, countless old and obsolete maps were used and then discarded: the idea that the Earth is at the center of the universe, the idea that disease is caused by bad odors in the air, or the idea that women's wombs would shrivel if they studied too hard—for example, by taking up a career in software development.

Another more serious problem is that your map is simply incomplete. Erik Sadberg-Diment wrote in 1985 in the *New York Times*, "But the real future of the laptop computer will remain in the specialized niche markets. Because no matter how inexpensive the machines become, and no matter how sophisticated their software, I still can't imagine the average user taking one along when going fishing." In this now amusing failed prediction, the key words are obvious: "I still can't imagine…"

A map is frequently fixed and unchanging and may well represent a picture of reality already passed. A mental model is our best guess for explaining how things work right now, given everything we know. Unfortunately, a map can never be smarter than we are, and it will contain all the biases and blind spots that we do.

Many people routinely fail to predict game-changing events because the models they have of the world are simply too small—they're incomplete and based on the *limited* knowledge they have in that moment. The trouble in holding a little too tightly to the map you have of the world is you just might miss amazing new information as it flies by you, blinded because you expected something different. The map, being an imperfect reflection of reality, is only meant to be temporary. Giving it a more permanent status will only lock you into ways of thinking that may not work.

Remembering this fact will mean you routinely give yourself the opportunity to step outside your perceptions and assumptions and re-evaluate the mental shortcuts you use to make sense of life.

What's the alternative to using a map to understand the territory? Simple: traveling the territory for real, in person! Trust your own direct experience before you trust a map, if possible.

Real, lived experience is incomparable. When you immerse yourself in reality as far as possible, really see it, feel it, taste it, and become curious about what it is without rushing in to explain it too quickly, your perceptions are greatly enriched. How many times have you taken someone else's opinions as fact? How many times has someone else told you how the world is, or how it works, and you accepted it without ever giving yourself a chance to verify this for yourself?

Obviously, direct experience isn't always possible. But it may nevertheless be useful to once in a while entertain a little doubt in the models you hold dear—what if you have an opinion right now that's as short-sighted as Erik Sadberg-Diment's views about computers? Paradoxically, the only way you can get closer to accurate, high-quality models of the world around you is to be willing to frequently question the ones you have and to drop those that aren't carrying their weight.

A map is necessarily a mere shadow of the thing it's pointing to. If a map were as big and complex as the world it was trying to explain, then it wouldn't be useful to us anymore as a model. Many people look to various maps of the world as though they were carved in stone. But consider that even seemingly rock-solid scientific theories like gravity or general relativity are models in precisely the same way as the idea that the universe revolves around the Earth was a model.

For a time, this "geocentric" assumption really did help explain the observed movement of the heavenly bodies. Our models today may well be better, and they may have more power in explaining phenomena around them, but several theoretical physicists have had success describing and understanding our universe using other, equally useful models. For some great thinkers, the entire construct of science itself is merely an admittedly useful paradigm that humans are particularly fond of at this point in history.

Science may fail to help us explain or understand certain psychological phenomena, but that doesn't mean they don't exist. That would be the mistake of trying to fit reality to match the map. Rather, another, different map can be used to help us make sense of the psychological territory. It's rather like needing one kind of map for exploring deserts and an entirely different one for exploring the depths of the ocean.

Remembering that the map is not the territory is a simple but powerful way to remind yourself of why you're using mental models in the first place: not to replace reality, but as a temporary tool to better understand it. You can use this principle in practically every area of your life. The next time you're facing some difficult problem or have trouble making sense of your choices or limitations, ask yourself these questions:

- What assumptions are you making about what you're experiencing? Have you told yourself a story that explains your situation, and is this story strictly accurate?

- In understanding that you're using a mental map, do you understand the map's limitations or have you been acting as though it had none?
- When you observe the world around you, do you often find information that conflicts with your pet theories? What does this say about the quality of your models?

By asking yourself these questions, you step outside of your mental models for a while to appraise their performance in your life. Let's consider an example. Maybe you've always been interested in psychological theories and have a bit of a habit of diagnosing those around you in an attempt to understand their behavior. Let's say you've come out of a particularly distressing breakup and now view your ex in a very specific way: you feel that they were in fact a *psychopath* and targeted you because you were a kind-hearted person.

You build a narrative around this "diagnosis"—you look at their behavior and explain it in terms of a grand psychological theory that checks all the boxes of a cruel, calculating individual who lacks empathy. You probably can imagine that there are some powerful defense mechanisms at play here, but for now let's just look at this "map" you're using to make sense of this painful breakup.

When you see evidence of your ex demonstrating remorse (which would suggest that they *weren't* a psychopath) you decide that this is actually them displaying an incredible ability to lie and manipulate (which would suggest that they *were* a psychopath). When your ex apologizes and tries to reconnect, you see evil intent—they are obviously trying to control you. But then when they eventually move on, you interpret this as proof that they are cold-hearted and never wanted to give the relationship a real chance.

This may all seem very obvious when laid out this way, but many people do some version of the above with very little self-awareness. Let's consider the questions above:

What are the assumptions being made, and is the story strictly accurate? If the person in our example is honest with themselves, they would see that they've gone far beyond assumptions and into a foregone conclusion. They've made their decision about what's true, and are looking for evidence after the fact to support their belief. The story may or may not be accurate, but only a professional can make that diagnosis, and anyway, what does it matter if they *are* a psychopath?

Our person could ask whether there were any limitations in their chosen map, i.e. the model where they pathologize their ex using trendy psychological concepts. Of course, they can only do this if they're aware that a model is being employed in the first place. Again, honesty and self-awareness might allow our person to see that there are several competing (and more elegant) theories to explain the behavior—i.e., people behave poorly sometimes when relationships end, or even the simpler "my ex is just a jerk." The psychopath concept is one that is heavily criticised and debated even amongst professional psychologists and psychiatrists—a good clue is that "psychopath" itself is not a recognized mental disorder in the DSM, but something you're more likely to see on a true crime TV series.

Finally, is there any information that conflicts with the chosen model? Here, we can remember Darwin's golden rule and get real about whether challenges to our dominant worldview have some merit. This would be all the evidence that is selectively ignored or twisted, such as the ex demonstrating remorse and empathy.

Of course, you won't always be showered with counterevidence every time you hold a less-than-ideal mental map of the world, and often you may be actively praised for it (we don't even need to list examples here!). But it's good practice to nevertheless keep your eyes open for evidence—even and especially evidence that you don't like.

The above line of questioning can be understood as a rudimentary form of experiment. It's the habit of testing our assumptions, and exposing them to different treatments to see the outcome.

Does our model stand up to scrutiny? Does it work in context A as well as it does in context B? Why or why not? We look a bit more closely at this experimental way of thinking in the next section.

The value of conducting thought experiments

There was a time when mankind knew so much less about the world. We take so much of what's around us as a given, forgetting where it came from. Look around you and you'll see that almost everything was, at some point, discovered or created by some enterprising or curious human being. The devices you use daily, the symbols making up the language you're reading right now, the mechanics of the electricity powering your home, all the medical marvels that went into keeping you alive and well in this moment... (Ignore the fact that someone once had to look at a cow and decide "I will try to drink whatever comes out of these pink things.")

Each of these accomplishments had to be fought for and won, one tiny step at a time.

Much of what our modern world is made of comes directly from the diligent effort of people working to understand the universe—and create their own inventions. All this scientific and technological progress was made not simply by sheer force of will or strength, but by using the scientific method, and prioritizing rational argument founded on sound empirical or logical data. In other words, *the experiment* is a mental tool so immense, so valuable, and so central to the survival of our species that it's hard to imagine where we'd be without it. It takes us from point A to point B, and it lets us know that we are directly affecting the world we inhabit.

Instead of cowering in the face of the unknown, experiments allow you to systematically and logically ask questions of the world around you, and make sense of the answers. It's a tool to gradually pull back ignorance and reveal useful facts and information, unearth new possibilities, or show us where we've made an error.

Of course, in this classical view, you may be thinking of the quintessential "experiment":

a scientist in a lab poking around with test tubes or wires, or a clinical trial for a new medication. The truth is, we conduct experiments all the time, formally and informally, consciously and unconsciously. Any time we deliberately manipulate conditions around us and carefully note the outcome, we are doing an experiment. Granted, not every experiment is going to be rigorous or perfectly sound! Nevertheless, experimentation is a method of patterning and understanding our encounters with the world. The concept behind this book is that some of the best experiments *can be done with nothing more than your mind.*

Eons ago, humans had to learn things the hard way: if you wanted to know if a berry was poisonous or not, you ate it and hoped for the best. But, if you survived, everyone could learn from your actions without having to incur any risk themselves. Gradually, people could build on what they already knew so that less and less had to be done concretely, out there in the world.

Thought experiments are conducted in a similar spirit. If we explore new ideas, arguments and scenarios *mentally* rather than literally, we're freed from so many limitations. What would be impossible or impractical to do physically is accomplished with nothing more than careful thought.

Thought experiments are not subject to any moral or natural laws, can be done relatively quickly and have (for the most part!) no real-world consequences. Their strength is that they give us the opportunity to fully flesh out certain hypothetical possibilities without committing to them practically. They allow us to discover aspects of ourselves we might not have otherwise, and consider the ramifications of certain possible acts long before we are technologically capable of them. There are countless innovators who, if asked where their inspiration came from, will point to speculative sci-fi from centuries prior, or whimsical "what-if" questions that spurred their curiosity.

The thought experiments we'll be exploring in this book have all served a particular purpose in their historical context. However, in learning about them, we teach ourselves to reach outside our own habitual thoughts and beliefs. What philosophy in general, and thought experiments in particular, can teach us is twofold: firstly, that we are inhabiting a *way* of thinking at all, and secondly, that our way of thinking can be changed.

As you read on, the hope is that you'll develop your own critical thinking skills, mental agility and self-awareness. You'll get comfortable *thinking about thinking*—perhaps the most valuable and transferable skill there is! By learning to carefully consider the virtues and drawbacks of the very process of thinking itself, you give yourself the opportunity to spot bias, question assumptions, more deeply understand your beliefs and—if you're lucky—open the door to a completely new idea.

Thought experiments are like a grand arena where you can take your brain out to play, to explore and to learn about itself, to grow larger and more robust. The ability to see not just *what is* but also *what could be* is fundamental to any endeavor that requires creativity or problem-solving acumen. It also helps you shift perspectives if necessary and consider something we seldom do: that we might be wrong! Manipulating thoughts, information, multiple variables, and coming up with an answer (for which there is no true right or wrong—a learned ability in itself) is something that can be applied to every walk of life.

Throughout history, thought experiments have allowed great thinkers and philosophers to see beyond their immediate grasp, to ask far-ranging questions and push the limits of human knowledge. Using thought experiments in your own life will make you a more focused, robust thinker with a cognitive and intellectual scope far wider than if you'd never challenged yourself in this particular way.

Finally, perhaps the most important benefit to engaging in thought experiments is that you give yourself the chance to chew over questions for which there simply *isn't* an answer, even with infinitely advanced scientific, technological or philosophical tools. Training your brain to confidently engage with these sorts of questions is enriching beyond the quick satisfaction of solving a problem or optimizing what you already know.

So, let's look a little closer: what exactly constitutes a thought experiment? Is it merely a question, simply asking "what if?"

Well, yes and no. The spark of wonder and curiosity is certainly the beginning, but a well-conducted thought experiment is also about the careful analysis of your answer, of other peoples' answers, and how to interpret them.

A big part of a thought experiment is thoroughly considering the consequences and implications of certain conditions, actions or choices. It's more along the lines of, "What happens IF such-and-such is true?" Thought experiments are completely fabricated "conditionals"—they are fictions which can obliquely bring us around to truths, or at the least illuminate our limitations, assumptions or errors. A truly great thought experiment often spurs further questions—a sign that your mind is mentally exploring an entirely new theoretical space. You may come across surprising answers and the opportunity to completely change your worldview—without the bother of having to actually *do* anything!

Thought experiments require us to apply our imagination, to entertain hypotheticals, and follow through potential outcomes and ramifications without actually trying them out for "real." When people encounter new scientific, political or cultural developments, they extrapolate and may start to think about possible future worlds—for instance, what would it look like if the DNA for every plant was owned by a corporation? If we take some commonly held tenets and follow them to their full conclusion, where do we land?

In our mind's eye, we see our best guess of the outcome, or a predicted conclusion, modeled on what we know now. We take our time to contemplate circumstances that aren't the case, can never be the case, or which we don't wish to be the case. Essentially, a thought experiment allows us to carry out "tests," but in the laboratory of our minds.

The Problem of the Runaway Trolley

Consider a seemingly simple hypothetical situation: You are watching a train that's headed right for five people tied to the tracks, who will certainly be killed if the train continues. If you pull a lever, the train will divert and head down another track, killing instead just a single person tied to that track. So, if you fail to act, five people die, but if you do act, only one person dies. The question is, would you pull the lever? Why?

Now, the idea is not to say, "That would never happen, so who cares?" The situation, obviously, is contrived. But it forces us to think outside the box and take a closer look at our default mental models. It invites us to have a conversation beyond what is immediately and concretely in front of us.

Simply by asking the question, you have participated in one of philosophy's classic thought experiments, the so-called Trolley Problem. You may be spurred to think all kinds of new thoughts, strengthening different modes of reasoning just as an athlete trains different muscles of their body.

You may wonder, if we think a single life is important, does this imply that five lives are five times as important? Here you're grappling with utilitarianism. You may believe most people would act to minimize harm if given the chance, considering what you know of how people normally behave (deductive reasoning), or you may wonder if not acting in this case completely absolves a person of guilt (now you're thinking about moral philosophy).

You may wonder, what if the single person was your child or parent? What if you had to physically push a person in front of the train to stop it? What if each of the five people had cancer and was going to die within the next year? What if there were five babies, yet the lone person standing was akin to Albert Einstein or some other genius? What if you had the power to sacrifice yourself in their places? What plea would you make if you were the single person? Now you're practicing switching perspectives and views.

If you ask yourself whether saving a family member versus a stranger is any more ethical, you're actively seeking and evaluating support for this argument. You might think the whole situation over and decide that it's implicitly acceptable to do wrong if it prevents a larger wrong from occurring. Congratulations—you've made a hypothesis. You could "test" this hypothesis (not an opinion) by asking whether pulling the lever should result in being punished by the law. You could make a prediction about what would happen if this was actually the case, in the real world, and on and on…

As you can see, one hypothetical situation can stimulate a whole new world of critical thinking, in every direction.

In fact, people have been chewing over the trolley problem for years, teasing apart what it can tell us about how humans think about culpability, the value of human life, moral behavior and psychology, the limits of a utilitarian approach in philosophy, and more. Many variants have been dreamt up too—for example, what if the single person was a villain?

While such thought experiments might seem glib—and perhaps a little unsettling—they do serve a useful purpose. Philosophers use these hypothetical situations to investigate what beliefs we hold to be true and, as a result, what kind of knowledge we can have about ourselves and the world around us. Sometimes, that process will be a little bizarre or unpleasant. But sometimes, it can also push us beyond our limits and open up new and different perspectives.

Long story short, thought experiments teach us to think.

Mastering second-order thinking

When faced with the need to make a decision, most of us only consider the immediate impact that decision will have—

especially if it's a time-sensitive or urgent one. We think in terms of one domino ahead; yet real life is never so simple and quarantined. What about the rest of the dominoes? They don't simply disappear.

We perceive most of our everyday decisions as isolated situations that don't have a ton of consequences, positive or negative. We practice a disturbing lack of foresight on a daily basis because that's how we're biologically wired as humans, and yet our instincts don't serve us very well here. Typical human thinking cannot be faulted: I step on a nail, and I jump to the side in pain and end up falling off a cliff. It just happens.

This is generally known as first-order thinking, and it is where we focus exclusively on resolving a question or decision at hand and don't consider the more long-lasting ramifications or how our decision will play out in the distant future. If it helps, call it *first-domino thinking*. The problem with this mode of thinking is that it is largely based on intuition, emotions, and convenience. The goal of first-order thinking is instant gratification, and sometimes this can be really useful. If you want to figure out what to eat for breakfast when you're in a rush, where to meet a friend, or which suit to wear to the office, this type of thought saves us from overanalyzing and allows us to make a choice quickly. As such, first-order thinking is useful when there isn't a bad choice you can make. You can meet your friend at a diner, at one of your houses, maybe at a bar, it doesn't really matter. Similarly, if you're picking a suit to wear for work, it's hard to go wrong.

Many of our decisions, however, especially the ones we toss and turn over at night, have consequences that extend beyond what we can see right before us. In terms of consequences, humans are as blind as bats. Small decisions one might make could lead to effects down the road they didn't foresee, resulting in a sort of butterfly effect. The outcome isn't limited to the immediate changes we've decided upon—other people or situations can be affected as well. Some of them may have been truly unpredictable, and some might be invisible until they rear their ugly heads. Others, though, only catch us by surprise because we didn't think the situation through quite deeply enough.

Okay, you've heard enough about what *not* to do, so what *should* we do? Visualize all the dominoes, otherwise known as *second-order thinking*.

This is simply trying to project into the future and extrapolate a range of consequences that you can use to conduct a cost-benefit analysis for your decisions or solutions. Instead of merely being satisfied about buying a new apartment, think about what it means for your credit, debt, and ability to own a huge dog in the future. Instead of bleaching your hair every week, consider that your bald spots have been increasing due to the harsh bleach and that a toupee may soon be necessary.

Second-order thinking has the usual effect of making you think twice about what you're doing and helps eliminate rash decisions, as you might expect when you consider the prolonged aftermath of your choices. It's the practice of seeking out as much information as possible to make measured decisions.

What's the first domino to fall after a decision? Now what are the three paths that first outcome can lead to? And where do those lead? You simply don't stop your analysis once the most obvious situations are articulated. Instead, you consider as many long-term, possible ramifications as you can. How will your decision cause other dominoes to fall? If you tip this domino, which other dominoes will you be unable to tip because of time or effort (opportunity cost)?

Famous investor Howard Marks provides a dead simple way this can apply to daily life:

> A good example can be seen in the hypothetical newspaper contest John Maynard Keynes wrote about in 1936. Readers would be shown 100 photos and asked to choose the six prettiest girls, with prizes going to the readers who

chose the girls readers voted for most often. Naive entrants would try to win by picking the prettiest girls. **But note that the contest would reward the readers who chose not the prettiest girls, but the most popular.** Thus the road to winning would lie not in figuring out which were the prettiest, but in predicting which girls the average entrant would consider prettiest. Clearly, to do so, the winner would have to be a second-level thinker. (The first-level thinker wouldn't even recognize the difference.)

This can be carried one step further to take into account the fact that other entrants would each have their own opinion of what public perceptions are. Thus the strategy can be extended to the next order and the next and so on, at each level attempting to predict the eventual outcome of the process based on the reasoning of other agents.

"It is not a case of choosing those faces that, to the best of one's judgment, are really the prettiest, nor even those that average opinion genuinely thinks the prettiest. We have reached the third degree where we devote our intelligences to anticipating what average opinion expects the average opinion to be. And there are some, I believe, who practice the fourth, fifth and higher degrees." (Keynes, *The General Theory of Employment, Interest and Money*, 1936).

Think about it this way: very rarely does something happen with no chain of events to follow. It's your job to look past the positive reinforcement and gratification you may receive, which frankly may be blinding you, and understand what could go wrong, how wrong it could go, and why it might have a negative outcome. What if you viewed each decision as having the potential to topple fifteen other dominoes, and then set about identifying them? *Tedious yet informative.*

Second-order thinking allows you to project the totality of your decisions. Even if you don't change your decision because of what you determine through second-order thinking, you think through ten times as many scenarios and thus make far more informed choices than you would otherwise. Sometimes, that's the best we can do as a person. We can't predict the future, but we can't not think about it.

If second-order thinking's so great, then why doesn't everybody do it? Because it's hard. Most of us do not want to spend the time to consider all the pros and cons of an action; we want to do what feels right and seems like it'll help us achieve our end goal. Humans aren't a shining example of doing the right thing on a consistent basis. Just look at our diets and how much money the weight-loss industry generates on an annual basis. Questioning how our actions will affect situations beyond what's right in front of us takes probing into the unknown and leads one into a labyrinth of thinking that can be strenuous or complicated. Other people might say we're "overthinking" a decision or problem.

The fact is, second-order thinking allows you to think clearly—at least more clearly than your competition. Most of the time, that matters. Nobody ever rises above average through making the obvious choices or accepting the most convenient, simplest answers. Being able to project and foresee happenings on a deeper, futuristic level is a hallmark of successful people and almost always turns out to be worth the extra effort. Adopting this mental model will improve your decision-making and stop letting things slip through the cracks.

To think in a second-order fashion, Howard Marks provides some guiding questions.

How broadly will this decision affect things in the future? What will your decision do beyond change your immediate concerns? What new concerns will be *created*? Will your decision's purpose be fulfilled?

Which result do I think will happen? Think beyond the simple resolution of the most immediate problem: if you take this course of action, what effect will it have if it succeeds or fails? What do those outcomes look like? What do semi-success and semi-failure look like? This naturally leads to the next question.

What are the chances that I will succeed or be right? From as objective a standpoint as possible, what is the probability that your assessment is accurate? Is your prediction realistic or at least a little steeped in fantasy or paranoia? Every decision has a cost-benefit ratio to it. Are you too openly courting failure or semi-failure?

What does everybody else think? Hopefully you have access to at least one or two people—optimally more—who will give you an honest opinion about your prediction and whether they think you're on the right track or not. Although you shouldn't be unduly swayed by popular opinion, it's beneficial to know how your forecast is received. Consensus in numbers isn't generally something to strive for, but on the other hand, a complete lack of touch with reality is usually arrived at alone, with no second opinions, so you are really just trying to prevent the latter.

How is what I think different from everyone else? What are the prime splitting points between what you think and what popular knowledge and opinion dictates? What specific aspects of your information and prediction are different and why? What are they based on? What could you be missing? And again, this line of questioning naturally leads to the final point.

What dominoes do other people visualizing falling? Regardless of whether you actually have someone to bounce your ideas off of, the point of this last question is to step out of your own biased perspective and view decisions as other people would. Actively seek out and articulate the domino chain that other people might visualize, and see how the dominoes fall from their perspective. Not all perspectives are valid, but this tactic gives you more information to ultimately help you make the right choice.

Remember, this mental model's purpose is to expose and inform. We can't circumvent our human instinct of jumping to conclusions and deciding on a whim entirely, but we can be a bit more methodical about decision factors.

This mental model very well could have been named "Ignore the Monkey's Paw," but that seemed unnecessarily morbid. So instead, I'll just briefly recount the origins of the Monkey's Paw, and you can decide for yourself which title is more effective in forcing you to examine secondary consequences.

"The Monkey's Paw" is a short story written by W.W. Jacobs in 1902. It's about a man who finds a blessed (or cursed?) monkey's paw, which will grant him three wishes. Little does the man know that even though each wish will be *technically* fulfilled, there will be harsh consequences.

For his first wish, the man wishes for $200. The next day, his son is killed at work, and the company gives the man $200 as payment. For his second wish, he wishes for his son back. In a short amount of time, he hears a knock at the door, and when he peers outside, he discovers that it is his son's mutilated and decomposing body. Frightened beyond belief, his third wish is for his son to disappear. Unintended consequences matter!

Perspective is a tool
Thought experiments, second-order thinking and learning to distinguish between the map and the territory are all valuable tools in the meta-inventory you can use to master your grip on reality. You may have noticed that much of what has been discussed in this chapter overlaps in interesting ways—for example, the psychological affects the cognitive, which then impacts the decisions taken and

actions made, which feeds back into the psychological. Many of the approaches we've discussed above come with their own implied worldview and attitude—and in fact, we can approach many of these tools from either their mental and intellectual aspects or their psychological and attitudinal ones.

Mental models, then, are not just cognitive tools, but complete *tools of perception*. In changing our mindset and emotional landscape, our thoughts and perspective changes. In altering our thinking process, we see our emotions and beliefs adjust in turn. Rather than seeing your personality, outlook or overall character as something fixed and non-negotiable, you can start to look at it as a large, complex lens to view your world through.

For example, we've already alluded to the perspective of the scientist when we discussed thought experiments. The scientist's attitude is to encounter the unknown with curiosity and a drive to master uncertainty by gaining *understanding*. A scientist seeks to know why and how phenomena unfold as they do, and their perspective is a miniature, internalized version of the scientific method in general.

A controlled experiment sets up two or more conditions and manipulates one or more identified variables to then observe the outcome. Using logic, inferences can be drawn about the conditions, the groups tested, or the action taken by the scientist. In this way, hypotheses (which are essentially formal questions asked of the unknown) are supported or disproven. In fact, proving and disproving are not symmetrical; science proceeds solely by proving the null hypothesis—evidence that the ego and wanting to be right has no place in the scientific method!

But none of this is to say that scientists are the ultimate arbiters of reality. Other viewpoints may be just as useful or more so. The artist's perspective, for instance, prioritizes creativity. Artists don't identify variables and try to control for them. They are not concerned with constraints of any kind—they want to explore and innovate, play, create and do the unexpected. Uniqueness and beauty are undoubtedly the right lenses to use for some of life's problems—as evidenced by the fact that our greatest leaders are seldom described as "in the box" thinkers.

There are countless perspectives. You could think like an engineer, a businessman, a parent, an investigative journalist, a doctor, a historian, a mathematician, a programmer, a comedian, an art critic, a philosopher or an economist (god forbid!). Rather than any one being more correct or valid than the others, it's more about choosing just the right color palette for the picture you want to paint (from an artist's perspective, anyway!).

You could opt for the perspective of a designer or architect. This is the mindset that looks at the unknown and asks what it could *potentially* be. People using this approach build and develop new things, first by making scale models of the vision they want to create, and then tackling the details to bring their dream to life. This is an active, purposeful and future-oriented perspective that is not concerned with understanding or appreciating so much as it is with *making*.

Like the artist, designers play with concepts to find new possibilities, but they do so with an eye to ending up with a real-world result. This is an empowering mindset to adopt when you want to fully explore your agency, take charge and find practical solutions inside the parameters you're given.

Or you could forget about all of that and direct your conscious attention to something else entirely: the inner worlds of others. If you have the perspective of a teacher, psychologist or even politician, a working model of what's going on in other people's minds is essential. This ability to understand that others occupy a completely different set of mental models is called "theory of mind."

Salespeople, too, need to understand and even anticipate other people's needs and desires, and know how to speak to them. Teachers make a model of where their students' current understanding is and adjust their communication to help them comprehend what they currently don't. Psychologists use models of their own to understand, essentially, the models of others—and in fact much of the material in this book was written from within this perspective.

Understanding all these different possible perspectives has two advantages. Firstly, you're less likely to get stuck in any particular one and lose sight of other possibilities, and secondly, you give yourself almost endless scope to see and engage with your world. Think of it as handles on reality. Which mental model or perspective is the "right" one? The one that gets you the result you want.

In the beginning of our book we spoke about the difference between crystalized vs. fluid intelligence, and how it's not what you know, but how you think. Rather than learning "facts" (i.e. gathering data or knowledge), you equip yourself with something more flexible and useful: different ways of seeing. As you encounter novel situations in life, you don't need to scan for any stored information. You don't need to have any experience or expertise at all. You simply need to be proficient at inhabiting the most useful mental model or way of thinking in the moment. If you can do this, you've achieved the most valuable thing of all: you have *learnt how to learn*.

Takeaways

- It's not enough to remove obstacles to our clear thinking; we also need to make sure that the way we appraise reality is actually accurate. A mental model is a representation of reality, but the "map is not the territory" and we need to remember that models are necessarily simplified. We need to consistently examine our model's limitations and assumptions by asking ourselves questions and following Darwin's golden rule. Once we find that our model is incomplete, we must take active steps to stop using the same mode of thinking.
- Thought experiments are a useful tool for thinking about our beliefs, assumptions, and various hypotheses we come up with while tackling routine

issues in our lives. They can help us hypothetically test out our assumptions, and follow through on hypotheses set by our models. The way we do this is by taking our beliefs and assumptions to their logical conclusion and critically examining everything that is implied or follows from the line of thought we considered in our experiment.
- There are two levels of thinking, first and second-order thinking. First-order thinking is largely superficial and seeks to resolve or answer any question/issue we face based on our intuitive leanings. Second-order thinking entails seeing consequences and possibilities beyond the immediate present, especially during decision-making. In the former, the goal is simply to make a choice, whereas in the latter it is to make an informed, well-thought-out one.
- Different perspectives and worldviews are tools to help us achieve our goals. We can adopt the mindset of an artist, scientist, psychologist, designer, etc. to help us access different aspects of reality—each has its virtues when used consciously.

Chapter 3. How to think critically and determine truth

In an earlier chapter, we saw that "it's not what you think, but how you think." In this chapter, we're going to adapt this slightly to, "If you know how to think, nobody can tell you what to think."

So far, this book has been concerned with understanding the difference between knowledge and thinking, the importance of removing obstacles to clear thinking, and the value in learning to shift perspective to serve our needs and goals. Essentially, we have identified the target and the means—we have decided the destination we're travelling to and the kind of car we need to drive to go in that direction. Think of this chapter as a more detailed exploration of the literal nuts and bolts that make up that car.

Knowing how to properly support and argue any claims you make, to think logically, and to critically navigate your way around other people's claims is a skill that can and should be developed. Sadly, it only takes one look at the world we live in today to see that the skills of civil discourse, debate and critical thinking are in crisis.

Yes, it's all about learning to "think for yourself" and make sure that you don't just believe everything you're told. But, importantly, it's also about adopting a set of intellectual standards for *yourself*. As we've seen, getting at the truth of any matter has nothing to do with trumping our "opponents" or giving our ego a boost. It also goes beyond finding a bit of cleverness to get an edge in the workplace or in our studies.

Rather, becoming a deep and sophisticated thinker is a reward in itself. Before we embark on gaining mastery over the tools of argument, we need to consistently remind ourselves of one thing: our goal is to develop clear perception, logic, understanding, curiosity and insight... It isn't to "win."

Thinking, step by step
When you were asked to write essays in school or university, you were probably tasked with constructing a persuasive argument to back up this or that claim. The real exercise, however, is to consistently use this method even within ourselves and against our own most cherished assumptions.

Academic discourse and essays are simply more formal versions of what we're really interested in—everyday critical thinking. Everyone has an opinion. Everybody thinks and believes certain things. When you engage in critical thinking, however, you're asking certain statements or claims to *earn their keep*. You expect a little more from yourself.

When you can reflexively look at the arguments you're employing and see their strengths and weaknesses, they automatically become your tools, and you can use them at will; if you stay locked inside a particular argument, however, you are always subject to its flaws or blind spots. You are always at a disadvantage because you never experience one of the greatest opportunities: the chance to change your mind.

So, how does one argue?

How should we pattern and organize our thinking?

Many of us begin with what we want to prove and then work backwards. In other words, decide what you want to be true and then construct an argument to make it so! Hopefully if you've read this far, you can immediately see why this is the wrong way around. Think of a statement or claim as a privilege you earn only after you've undertaken a degree of data-gathering.

The best ideas are those that are thoroughly *developed*, so for step one of this process, try to empty your mind completely and appraise the data in front of you with fresh eyes. Without attempting to push a conclusion this way or that, simply understand what information exists. Take on the perspective of a student first, curious about the how, why and what.

Don't go into data-gathering with an agenda. In fact, don't cling to any conclusion to begin with, so you can freely sample information from a range of sources. Look for repeating patterns or interesting connections. Let the data simmer around in your head for a while and suggest questions to further guide your research.

What you want is to become very familiar with the topic, the current issues, the history, the terminology and methodological frameworks, the conflicts and controversies, the unanswered questions, the invested parties. At this point, you don't need to form any opinions. Depending on what situation you find yourself in, simply listen to others share their claims, read up on your topic, examine the literature or have a look at what facts you can gather—possibly taking notes.

As you research, allow the data to suggest questions and further avenues to explore.

Do you notice anything that's missing?

Do you see any conflicting statements?

Do you have any questions or things you'd like to understand better?

What is the general argument being presented? Can you see the broad strokes?

What evidence is in front of you?

What is the perspective or approach adopted by those making the argument? Why?

What vested interests are behind the data you're taking in? Is it neutral? Fact or opinion?

You are in scout mode now, totally curious and receptive. Obviously, you do need some basic standards as you gather information. You don't need to thoughtfully listen to someone who is being abusive or take in information from a source you already have reason to believe is not credible. But you can note these things and move on. Since you won't be able to do a complete sweep of *all* the information out there, you need to make sure you're getting the highest quality, most trustworthy sources possible, for a comprehensive view.

Only *after* you feel like you've covered enough ground can you move on to step two and start to formulate your own hypothesis. Keeping the scientific method in mind, a claim should ideally be defensible—i.e., it should be able to be proven or disproven. The scientist Karl Popper has written extensively on how unfalsifiable arguments, i.e. those that cannot be proven or disproven, make for bad science because they cannot be empirically verified and are not open to any new evidence that might emerge. You might have noticed that almost all conspiracy theories rely on unfalsifiable arguments, which is what makes people fall into the trap of believing them.

An example of this is the claim "Loch Ness is home to a monster." There's nothing one can do to disprove this statement because no matter what you say, the possibility of the Loch Ness monster existing remains. Arguments and hypotheses need to be possible to engage with intellectually to determine their veracity. In other words, a claim is more than an opinion or preference. You might sincerely think, for example, that everyone in the field is reprehensible and the topic is boring—but this is neither here nor there.

The easiest way to make sure that your claim is defensible is to acknowledge the counterargument from the outset, i.e. "*even though* many people believe you should drink eight glasses of water a day, I haven't seen much peer-reviewed evidence to suggest that's true." It should also be said that there's no point going through this process if there genuinely is no argument about your particular claim, and in looking at the data you find no gaps or disagreements.

Taking on a stance is something that many people in the modern world believe is a divine, unalienable right, i.e. "you are entitled to your opinion." While true, it may be better to say, "None of us are entitled to claim an opinion is fact." Once you make a claim, it is still nothing more than a claim. This means two things: firstly, that if you encounter other people's claims, you are under no obligation to accept them as fact, and secondly, that other people are under no obligation to accept yours.

What elevates a claim is the existence of evidence. Importantly, this isn't to say we need *proof*. One needs only to consider the pains taken to ensure fairness in a court of law or the decades it takes for the scientific community to arrive at a roughly established theory to appreciate that proof is a luxury. Rather, you need to support your position adequately.

Many people assume that a claim is enough on its own. When their position is challenged, they will simply repeat their position, not realizing that shouting louder or getting more emotional doesn't add anything to the validity of the argument. But evidence, by its nature, contains no opinion or guesswork.

This is not to say you can never make a claim unless it's accompanied with a fifty-page thesis outlining all the evidence, only that it's worth being mindful of the status of various thoughts, opinions, beliefs and assumptions you hold. You need to explain to your interlocutor why it is reasonable to believe your claim over theirs on the basis of hard evidence like statistics, reasonability, and showing that your claim is more likely to be true (in the event that it cannot definitively be decided), instead of simply restating your position and expecting it to be self-explanatory. Likewise, be crystal clear about the information you encounter in the media, from others, from people in authority, and so on. Can you clearly tell the difference between an opinion, an absolute fact, an accepted "working theory," a guess, and a wish?

Remember that other people may practice all the same techniques of self-delusion we covered earlier. They may be using several defense mechanisms, or operating to protect their egos. They may be trapped in their own perspectives which deeply color their view. Finally, it's not the end of the world to *not* form a claim, if the data doesn't really support it. Sometimes the best and wisest thing a person can say is, "I don't know."

When constructing an argument, you need to think of it as a dialogue, whether you are literally discussing the idea with someone or not. Address not just one or two points, but look at as many angles as possible. Do you know and understand the counterargument? What is your response to those claims? This goes a little deeper than simply weighing up the pros and the cons. It's more like shining a very bright light into a room to make sure you've seen into every corner.

It takes courage and maturity to arrive at a point where you realize your argument is poor. Abandoning a claim is not a sign of weakness, but evidence of intellectual strength. After all, this is *why* you put it to the test in the first place—to see if it was up to scratch. As long as you are sharpening your powers of discerning fact from fiction, truth from lie, then you are on the right track, even if you feel as though you have even less to rely on than when you began!

If, however, you find some evidence, you still need to work to connect it to your claim. *How* exactly does it support your view? What does it prove and is that relevant? A little evidence is great, but is it enough? This step can be the trickiest of all, mostly because it's easy to grasp at evidence that is actually not applicable to your claim. For example, you may be trying to understand the safety of a new medical technique, and you find a YouTube video of a doctor discussing why they believe the treatment is unsafe. But this isn't great evidence if the doctor works in a different country, and in a completely different field than the one you're researching.

But that's not all that's wrong with this piece of evidence. A YouTube video is obviously not the same as a peer-reviewed article, a white paper from a trusted authority, an encyclopaedia or a reliable news source. It might seem silly, but it can be hugely illuminating to literally slow down and write down or say out loud what claim you are making, and how your evidence supports it. Look for gaps. Can you summarize the evidence and link it directly to your position, in just one or two sentences?

Using the Toulmin method
Another tool to assist with critical thinking and decision-making is called the *Toulmin method*. While argument mapping is a box and arrow design, the Toulmin method is

more linear in nature and does not necessarily take into consideration objections and rebuttal. Instead, it is geared toward explaining in great length every aspect of your argument. This method can certainly be useful when you do not want to engage in an argument but rather simply want your counterpart to "get it." The components of the Toulmin method consist of the following:

- Claim. The main point that you are trying to make.
- Grounds. The proof or evidence supporting your point.
- Warrant. The explanation or connection between the claim and the grounds.
- Backing. Justification for the explanation.
- Qualifier. The likelihood of the claim.
- Rebuttal. Exceptions or limitations of the claim.

And to be clear, each of the above elements must be addressed—this is how you can quickly evaluate the quality of an argument. Just like with argument mapping, the mere fact that you are forced to consider this checklist of elements can bring clarity in itself. As you define each component of your argument, remember that the ultimate goal is to analyze and think critically. Let's look at an example of how the Toulmin method could be used in an everyday situation.

- Claim: Cigarette smoking should be banned in the workplace.
- Grounds: Secondhand smoke is detrimental to the health of other employees.
- Warrant: Provide details of a study that describes how the inhalation of secondhand smoke in a work environment may inhibit brain function and therefore prevent employees from performing at their best.
- Qualifier: Indicate that although this may not occur in *all* employees who inhale secondhand smoke, it is possible that some employees' brain function may be inhibited.
- Rebuttal: Smoking is an addiction that may be difficult to break for many people, and providing a location for them to smoke is imperative.

In this case, although you have acknowledged the rights and habits of smokers, your claim is that smoking may cause problems for non-smokers and should be banned in the workplace. As you can see, you have touched briefly on the limitation of your claim since it is probably a highly controversial issue, yet you do not want to linger on this point. This method is much more effective and useful when used for complex arguments around which there may be high opposition, resistance, and dissent. Let's look at another example of how the Toulmin method can be used to break down an argument.

- Claim: In order to reduce the number of car accidents that occur as the result of texting, stricter laws should be in place to deter people from texting while driving.
- Grounds: According to the National Safety Council, 1.6 million accidents occur in the United States due to texting.
- Warrant: People who text while driving are distracted.
- Qualifier: Although accidents may still occur from other distractions, by

regulating texting, the number of accidents should be reduced.
- Rebuttal: Creating additional regulations for law enforcement to enforce will certainly place additional burdens on our police force. However, if it will save lives, the addition of manpower should be considered.

In this argument, you have clearly stated your case that texting causes distraction and therefore may result in accidents. In order to reduce the number of accidents and save lives, additional laws should be implemented and enforced.

Using the principle of *cui bono*
Let's briefly put on the perspective of a police detective, adopting the mental model wherein we investigate not just the facts, but the motivations and reasons behind them.

You've seen the story play out before: a mysterious murder occurs, and the criminal investigators ask an illuminating question—"Who benefits?" The Latin phrase is *cui bono*, and it speaks to a popular trope in both real and fictional courtrooms. The idea is that those who have the most to benefit from a certain event are most likely to be responsible for it. But this principle can also be applied to your reasoning and practice of critical thinking.

Think of it this way—the people most likely to gain something from a piece of disinformation are more likely to be the ones who spread it in the first place. Asking who benefits can help you locate the people behind new political legislature, a piece of ideology, an article, or even just a nasty rumor going around the office.

This principle is great to include in your intellectual inventory because it reminds you that as hard as you try to access neutral information, you live in a world populated by people with special interests that may or may not align with the truth—or your personal interests, for that matter. This simple question helps you look at a situation and ask *why* it unfolded as it did. For this you need to understand their position relative to yours, and what their motives are.

Once you dig into their perspective, you can start to unravel cause and effect relationships and gain insight into facts that may be hidden. Sadly, we don't live in a world where free, accurate and complete information is readily available to us. When we encounter information, there is an enormous chance it has been designed specifically with an agenda in mind.

Leaving aside the entire world of advertising for a second, there are now countless websites online that look and feel official and trustworthy, when in fact they are created by people with hidden agendas. Plenty of quackery is peddled in the name of medical science but is really nothing more than a veiled attempt to make money; many "public service announcements" or "reports" are likewise special ads designed by lobby groups to manipulate public opinion one way or another.

Cast a critical eye on opinion pieces in the media, or politicians trying to rally your support. You cannot be deceived or manipulated unless you are willing to race ahead and come to conclusions without thinking carefully about what's in front of you.

So, slow down and take your time. Assume nothing. Ask questions. Notice if someone is attempting to persuade you of anything in the first place. Why? How do they benefit from you agreeing with them? Always look deeper at the *backend* of people's arguments—remember, without evidence, a claim is just an opinion.

Obviously, we don't want to get tangled in paranoid conspiracy theory and start to doubt everything. This principle is a rule of thumb only, and not a guarantee. Sometimes, people spread misinformation because they themselves are misinformed or don't know better and refuse to educate themselves. The principle is not enough to be used alone; you need to consider other factors carefully. It can help you identify the simplest and most likely answer, sure, but it's not foolproof. To use a silly example, fish benefit from rising sea levels but probably aren't conspiring to make it happen!

The reverse is also true: people sometimes act even when they stand to gain nothing from doing so. What's more, just because you don't see or understand someone's motives, it doesn't mean they aren't there, powerfully driving their actions. Nevertheless, unpicking a situation in terms of benefits and motivations is a great way to gain insight. A variation on this maxim is "follow the money"—i.e. to understand what's going on in a situation, look at who benefits (financially). This is captured in the Latin term, *cui prodest*—who profits?

Assumptions—don't get tripped up
An argument is a story. Certain premises are put forward, and these build logically on one another to arrive at a sound conclusion. Someone may give you a handful of reasons (premises) to support the claim they want you to adopt (i.e. the conclusion of the argument). In other words, it's a referential exercise—"we believe X because of Y."

The quality of an argument comes down to the quality of its premises, and the way in which they've been stitched together, or the soundness and logic in the argument itself. The best way to analyze an argument made to or by you is to set the conclusion aside and focus exclusively on the premises, and identify the one premise which is the weakest. So, if I say that smoking is bad (premise 1), and we shouldn't do bad things (premise 2), hence we shouldn't smoke (conclusion), the weakest premise here is that we shouldn't do bad things. Why shouldn't we? Are there no circumstances under which doing a bad thing is justifiable? What about when you're trying to prevent a bigger wrong by committing a smaller wrong? Disputing the premise of a conclusion is the only way to disprove that conclusion. Intuitively, it makes sense that a conclusion is only as good as the information it relies on.

Learning to think clearly means becoming comfortable and familiar with all these elements of reasoning. When you encounter an argument (not a simple claim or unsupported opinion, but a persuasive argument), put on your architect's perspective and look at the scaffolding on which everything is built. Identify the final claim you are being asked to believe, as well as the evidence offered to support it.

You can then start to consider whether the evidence is all that good, and how well it supports the claim. You can also look at the internal logic of the argument and whether any fallacies have been committed. Entire branches of philosophy are devoted to this endeavor, and it's not something to master overnight.

But one very effective element to begin to work with is *assumptions*.

Remember that an argument is an artificial thing. It has been constructed especially for a purpose. The person making the argument is asking you to pay attention to some very particular selected pieces of information… but what haven't they included? The person making the argument is using mental models, just like you. And as you already know, a mental model is a simplification of reality. It necessarily cuts some detail out. What has the person making the argument missed or assumed in putting together the argument as they have?

Carefully considering an argument's assumptions is a great way to employ meta-cognition because it looks beyond the stated claims and into the thought processes that produced those claims. It looks, in other words, at the models that gave rise to the particular premises and the logical structure of the argument in question.

Intelligent people can be fooled by seemingly sophisticated, "rational" arguments that look perfectly true on the surface. This is because they only consider the visible, deliberate parts of the argument, and forget about the invisible, hidden ones. Just as unconscious forces can influence our thoughts and behaviors, unconscious beliefs and assumptions can color even the most "logical" arguments.

Don't just ask what claims an argument is making. Also ask what claims seem so obvious and natural that they didn't even need to be asserted at all. It's *here* that you may find the most interesting errors, omissions or even deceptions. Assumptions are embedded right into the very fabric of an argument, and take a deliberate shift in perspective to spot. In fact, one wonders how much of "objective fact" is actually accepted this way, quietly riding in on countless unspoken and unacknowledged assumptions.

Whether deliberately concealed or entirely unconscious, assumptions can hide anywhere. They're often hiding in that leap from the evidence to the conclusion. An assumption here is like a little invisible bridge that helps you reach a conclusion you wouldn't have otherwise, on the strength of the given evidence alone.

Look at the evidence itself. Ask, "What am I assuming to be true if I am to accept this piece of evidence or reason?" There may be a host of assumptions, but you're concerned with those that are necessary for you to consider a particular premise true.

Let's dig deeper and consider different types of assumptions: value assumptions and descriptive assumptions. A value assumption is when the person making the argument has an unspoken preference for one thing over another, and assumes that the listener does or at least should share this value, too. But without this assumption, the argument doesn't quite hold together.

Many intelligent people are surprised to find that those who agree with them actually do so for very different reasons. A person may make an impassioned appeal to you on the issue of abortion rights, or on whether religion should be taught in schools, or about the ethics of eating meat, but never explicitly tell you the values that inform these beliefs. For example, if someone makes an anti-abortion argument with premises that heavily rely on fundamental Christian concepts to support it, it's not likely to mean much to listeners who consider themselves atheists.

We all hold many values, however, and the relative proportion with which we rank them matters, too. You may value fairness and ethical work practices, but attach slightly more importance to the convenience of buying cheap items made in third-world countries. These relative values influence the arguments we make—and those we are receptive to.

The best way to see assumptions clearly is to... well, make no assumptions. Look for value conflicts (as distinct from conflicts in content or information) and see what is taken as a given for the argument to stand as it does. Look at how the argument lays out the consequences of certain actions or positions, to infer what values are being held. For example, if someone argues that blood sports like boxing should be banned because they result in lasting brain damage for the participants, you can guess they value personal health and well-being. At any rate, they have very different values from someone arguing against boxing because it competes with the pro-wrestling scene.

The trouble with identifying value assumptions out in the real world is that they are often couched as premises, reasons or evidence, when they aren't. It's worth teasing apart assumptions—even and especially when you actually happen to agree. Opinion pieces in trusted newspapers are packed with value assumptions; after all, this is what makes it possible to identify a publication as left or right leaning.

When you "read between the lines," you can see hidden assumptions everywhere. Consider coverage of the Covid-19 pandemic, and see if you can discern the difference between different authors' values. Look at the balance between the values of safety vs. liberty, the assumptions made about how much risk or discomfort is optimal, and even in the value of expert opinion vs. individual belief.

Value assumptions tell you what kind of world the speaker inhabits—i.e., what mental models or filters they're using. Begin with these and their stated argument will make more sense to you.

Descriptive assumptions, on the other hand, are built into the very reasons that are there to support a conclusion. A descriptive assumption is almost like a smaller argument folded into the bigger one. For example:

Premise: The overachieving A student has succeeded brilliantly all through school and university.

Conclusion: They will find a prestigious job and be successful.

The assumptions being made here are not value assumptions. Rather, the argument assumes that if a student performs well, they'll continue to perform well. Another assumption is that success in a school environment is comparable to success in the working world, and that achieving one means you will achieve the other. You can probably see other assumptions that the conclusion depends on, namely that there isn't a massive economic depression or that the student is actively seeking a job in the first place.

Descriptive assumptions are nothing more than unstated beliefs about how the world is (or should be). They tend to follow certain basic patterns—the one above makes the fallacy of assuming that "the past is a perfect predictor of the future." Other descriptive assumptions could include:

- "I'm a typical case," wherein a person argues for the belief that their preferences, worldview, priorities or beliefs are standard in all people;
- "My perspective matters," wherein the person and their worldview are at the center of the universe and other mental models are not acknowledged;
- "The world is a just place" or "What ought to be true will be true," wherein there is an unwavering belief in justice or fairness;
- "The individual decides," wherein it is assumed that everything in life comes down to personal choices alone.

If you find yourself questioning either value or descriptive assumptions, then you probably disagree with the resulting argument. In fact, many stalemates and long-lasting feuds exist not because one or the other side has incorrect or incomplete arguments, but rather that both sides are arguing from worldviews that are mutually unintelligible to the other.

If you cannot share assumptions, it's a little like being willing to play a football game together, but being unable to even agree on which field to play on. In fact, it would be almost impossible to have a fruitful conversation with someone who didn't value your right to speak, or to engage in an argument with someone whose very concept of "logical" clashed with yours.

Assumptions needn't always derail an argument, however; the premise of this book is that by becoming aware of the cognitive landscapes we inhabit and the thinking tools we use to navigate them, we can not only become better thinkers ourselves, but better able to recognize and work around weak, unreasonable or fallacious thinking in others.

Understanding our own assumptions, values, blind spots and beliefs empowers us to decide if we want to keep them, or make changes. It also helps us to understand *why* we disagree or agree with someone— beyond simply responding with knee-jerk emotion or habit. Let's return to the sentiment we began this chapter with, i.e. that the goal is not to win arguments, but to sharpen our mental machinery and bring a clear, critical attitude to the claims of others and our own as well.

This may seem like a lot to keep in mind every time you encounter an argument in real life (which is surprisingly often), but it boils down to just a few key questions:

1. Can I identify the topic and the conclusion/claim being made?
2. Can I identify all the reasons/premises/evidence offered to support that claim?
3. Can I identify any underlying value or descriptive assumptions?
4. Can I identify any flaws in logic or fallacies?
5. Is the evidence provided sufficient and good quality?

When you are faced with an op-ed in a newspaper, an advertisement or even a persuasive argument by a friend, pause for a second and run through these questions. Put on the perspective of an investigative journalist or even a judge hearing a case, and adopt the attitude of a scout merely seeking to understand the ins and outs of the information in front of him before he blindly accepts the conclusions.

Not only does critical thinking help you get to the beating heart of arguments, it also helps you analyze all information in front of you, including the things you need to consider when making an important decision. We'll briefly look at how to do this in the next section.

Smart questions to refine your decision-making

1. Consider your future emotions by imagining how you would feel about this decision in ten minutes, ten months, or ten years. This shifts your perspective in time, alerting you to whether you're giving too much weight to current emotions.
2. How will this decision affect your life as it pertains to long-term values? It's easy to identify what you value right now, but can you imagine what future-you values?
3. What options have you considered and ultimately

decided against? As above, it's always useful to consider counterarguments thoroughly.
4. To shake off your bias, try to build a case against your decision. Genuinely consider all contrary evidence.
5. What missing variables or information may help you make a better decision? Ask yourself what you don't know, or don't know yet. Can you suspend your decision until you have more information?
6. When you find yourself stuck, consider what other people have done in similar situations. Can you speak with them? It can be a great idea to leverage the experience of those who've already been through what you're going through.
7. Can you test your decisions at a small scale? By trying out something low-risk and quick first, you give yourself the opportunity to perform a mini-experiment before committing.

8. Since every resource (time, money, etc) can be put to alternative uses, every action, choice or decision has an associated opportunity cost. Can you identify the things you miss out on by making your particular choice? Is this sacrifice acceptable?
9. List out all the assumptions you have about the decision you're facing. Are they value or descriptive assumptions? Are they well-founded? What's the alternative?
10. Once you've defined all the typical assumptions around your decision, it's time to reverse your thinking and define the opposite of each. How might that change things?
11. Consider how you would advise a friend who faces a similar decision. What might you notice for them that you didn't for yourself? Take a close look at all the excuses and justifications that jump up to explain why you are *not* like your friend.

12. Who are the influencers of your decision? (e.g., family, friends, and colleagues). How much are you driving the decision versus those around you, and are you happy with this balance?
13. What would you expect to happen given all of the probabilities? Also consider what would happen if you did absolutely nothing.
14. On a scale of 1-10, rate the confidence in your decision (10-complete confidence). Also ask yourself what a comfortable level of uncertainty is for you. How much risk are you willing to incur for a possible gain?

Takeaways

- Thinking critically is the step-by-step process by which we process new data to arrive at well-supported conclusions—or else critically appraise the claims of others. By mastering this skill, we learn how to come up with compelling arguments and build coherent, well-informed worldviews that are not full of biases and rigid thinking. It also helps us analyze the

wealth of information we come across on a daily basis. A lot of what we read on the news, for example, is opinion disguised as fact, and critical thinking will help you segregate the two thoroughly.
- The Toulmin method is a way to formally identify your argument's claim, grounds, warrant, backing, qualifier and rebuttal. The claim is essentially your conclusion, the grounds are premises for the conclusion, warrant is an explanation of how and why the premises lead to the conclusion, while backing is proof that the premises are actually true. Qualifiers are any clarifications that need to be made, while rebuttals are answers to counterarguments.
- Assumptions are the biggest threat to critical thinking. We need to identify both descriptive and value judgments in our own and others' arguments so as not to be led astray. Value judgements are hard to reconcile because you can't really argue with someone who has a fundamentally different view of the world. However, descriptive judgements are essentially unqualified assumptions

that, when questioned, make the argument fall apart.
- Critical thinking can be used to assess our own thought processes and help us arrive at better decisions if we take the time to unpack our supporting arguments. If you have a certain belief, break it down into premises and conclusion, or the main claim and everything that supports it in your view. Think which premise is the weakest and consider whether it can be strengthened through proof or better analysis. If it cannot be, you have a belief that rests on weak arguments, in which case you should discard it and adopt a more rational outlook.

Chapter 4. How to think about your thinking

You may have read the questions in the previous chapter and thought to yourself, "*Wow, what a lot of hard work.*" Who has time to nitpick over details to that extent in the real world, where we have to make decisions quickly? Why not just "follow your gut" and let your intuition guide you some of the way?

It's a tempting (and popular) prospect. The world is complex and there isn't often time for analysis—so what about instinct? It's true that there's mounting scientific evidence for the many interesting ways the brain unconsciously makes decisions—i.e. how your intuition guides you.

But one thing hasn't really changed: as useful as it may be, intuition is simply not a *replacement* for rigorous critical analysis. Nothing is a genuine substitute for logic and reason, and in fact the more pressed for time you are and the more complex your decisions, the less you should assume that intuition alone is enough.

Intuition—not as trustworthy as it seems

We all like to believe that gut instincts hold some magical power. There's something appealing about it: you sit back and relax and your unconscious mind magically finds solutions for you, almost like a superpower. And haven't all of us experienced the strength of intuition before, or seen the positive results after following a hunch?

But this could be an example of pure confirmation bias—i.e., we remember all those instances where intuition paid off because they support our belief, all while conveniently forgetting about those times it *didn't* pay off. The less glamorous truth is that intuition and instinct are often little more than thinly veiled bias, prejudice or unexamined belief—the very things we've already seen can derail reason.

Our unconscious mind is as fallible as we are. It makes mistakes. Except these mistakes can be much more dangerous because they are not out in the open, where we can examine them closely. It's not a popular opinion, true, but human intuition can be irrational, unreliable, and downright nonsensical. The human need to find patterns is a wonderful thing—but what if those patterns are completely imagined, and all we see is what we want to see?

Intuition may be nothing more than the satisfying feeling of forcing unrelated new stimuli into old, fixed schemas and beliefs so we can make sense of them. It might *feel* right, but is it? Contrary to popular belief, intuition is even less reliable the more complex and chaotic the environment. After all, in the face of threat and chaos, we are more prone to falling back on safe assumptions and mental models that have worked in the past, instead of carefully picking our way through challenging new information.

Intelligent decision-making takes time. There's no way around it—only sustained, careful consideration of the objective facts can shed light on a problem... no matter how sure you already feel that you have discovered The Answer. In this chapter, we'll be looking at something a lot more difficult to cultivate than intuition: metacognition.

Instead of simply allowing our unconscious bias to run wild, we slow down and think about how we're thinking. Metacognition, in other words, is the skill of self-reflection and self-awareness. Where intuition is guided by self-interest and unexamined personal belief, metacognition seeks to stand outside of all this, to see the situation more clearly.

Metacognition—getting a handle on your own thoughts

Throughout this book, we've engaged in and encouraged metacognition, taking as a topic of thought the very process of thought itself.

When we practice metacognition, something special happens—we step *outside* of our thoughts. With a bird's-eye view on our own cognition, we find a degree of conscious control that isn't possible when we are fully identified with our thoughts, unable to see what we're doing and why. Metacognition is a powerful tool, because it shifts your perspective in a dramatic way: you are no longer in the passenger seat, being driven around by your beliefs and emotions; instead, you are behind the wheel.

Metacognition is a fundamental principle behind many methods of self-development, including cognitive-behavioral therapies. While we can become aware of *what* thoughts we have, we can also ask *how* those thoughts come about. Thoughts are informed by our perspective, our beliefs, and our mental models. And then, these thoughts influence our behavior and actions. Cognitive-behavioral therapy tries to use this perspective to not only understand thoughts, feelings and behaviors, but change them for the better.

Psychologist Albert Ellis introduced the "ABC model" which is still popular today. It's a simple way to help people rid themselves of unwanted beliefs, emotions and behaviors, by understanding how these three fit together.

Here's an example: Let's say someone walks into a room and everyone starts laughing. You can imagine the person immediately feels embarrassed and thinks, "Oh my god, they're all laughing at me, I'm such an idiot." They could then run out of the room again, angry and humiliated, and refuse to speak to anyone.

Because this person has low self-esteem, they interpret this outside event negatively, and assume people are laughing at them, when in fact someone happened to tell a joke at just the moment they walked into the room). You can see that the person's beliefs and feelings allowed them to interpret a triggering event in a particular way, and arrive at thoughts that are actually irrational.

Though the outside event certainly affected the person, it was really their *own* beliefs and resulting thoughts that created their experience, and shaped their subsequent behavior. The ABC model helps us understand how external events, thoughts, and emotions/beliefs connect, so we can make improvements going forward.

In the model, A is for activating event. In our example, this was the laughter. When we're using this model to examine our own lives, we can ask what triggered certain events, what happened, how it unfolded, who was involved, what role you played and how it felt.

B is for belief. This is our thoughts, feelings and mental models—conscious or unconscious—that occur in response to the activating event. In our example, the feeling of humiliation and the thought "I'm an idiot" are caused in a sense by the activating event, but the real culprit is an interpretation of objective events through personal filters, attitudes and perspectives.

The C in the model stands for consequences. Most simply, this is the behavior that results from both A and B, as well as a second wave of thoughts and feelings that might arise. What's more, the actions taken can themselves influence the environment and other people, feeding back into the cycle, reinforcing certain belief structures and patterns of behavior.

Now, there's nothing necessarily wrong with the way the ABC process unfolds. As human beings, we naturally respond to our environments, experience emotions, and act accordingly. The trouble occurs if our thoughts and feelings are irrational, or if how we think and feel brings consequences that are unwanted or harmful to us.

Beliefs can be anything—positive or negative, correct or incorrect, and any combination of these. For example:

A positive belief: My friends really like me.

A negative belief: Everyone secretly hates me.

A correct belief: Everyone laughed when I walked into the room.

An incorrect belief: Everyone laughed *because* I walked into the room.

A positive belief can be incorrect (hello, narcissism!) and a negative belief can actually be true. When you slow down and take the time to analyze this process in detail, however, you examine the beliefs you hold as objectively as possible. And this is why intuition can be dangerous—if we simply embrace our knee-jerk reactions to events, we never get the chance to look more closely at the underlying beliefs that drive them.

This means we can never get rid of faulty, irrational beliefs, and never change behavior we are actually unhappy with. In our example, the person may flee the room before anyone has a chance to explain what's happened. In bigger, more complex examples, leaving our beliefs and "intuitions" unexamined means we may trap ourselves in habits that don't serve us, unaware of how irrational and faulty thoughts, feelings and behaviors are reinforcing each other in a vicious cycle.

In real life, things are not this simple. We find ourselves in the middle of things and have to dive in somewhere, starting with a triggering event, or an emotion or even a final behaviour. Step by step, we can examine the situation at hand in terms of each of the three aspects, noting how each links into the other.

Where this model shines is its ability to zoom in on beliefs and thoughts that are incorrect, so that they can be replaced with more realistic ones. Then, according to the theory, the resulting consequences and beliefs can be updated to reflect the change. The main goal is to carefully evaluate how personal beliefs actually manifest in your life, through actions that are mediated through your emotions and thoughts.

As you can see, this is a very different approach from merely trusting "intuition." After all, how could we know the difference between a spontaneous thought, "I'm an idiot," and the strong gut feeling that all your friends hate you? Unless you analyze the situation clearly, you can't really know for sure. The wonderful thing about this model is that reminds us that the precipitating event is only ever a trigger—it's never the full cause. Instead, our experience largely comes down to our *own interpretations* of these events, according to our beliefs and mindset. It's all about those mental models.

Used consistently, the ABC theory might help the person in our example notice that certain core beliefs pop up often for them. They might see that they have a pattern of perceiving neutral stimuli as more judgmental and rejecting than they really are. When the person understands how this irrational thought stunts their behavior and causes them to limit themselves socially, they can start to make meaningful changes.

When we take our impulses, reactions and unexamined beliefs at face value, we never see what's underneath them. On further investigation, someone may well discover that their friends *do* actually dislike them. But even this outcome is preferable to merely assuming or fearing the worst, because you are still empowered to take conscious, rational action.

Our emotions are a part of life, and add color and meaning to our experience. There's no need to ignore them completely or to go about life like a robot. However, we are also blessed with critical faculties that allow us to reason about the world and our place in it. When we employ metacognition, we can understand emotion's place in the greater process.

A good way to start using the ABC model in your own life is to simply become aware of your thoughts, and what they tell you about the beliefs you hold. Awareness is the first step in metacognition. For example, a car could cut you off in traffic and you could instantly notice anger flaring up inside you. Take a breath, and notice what thoughts you have:

"That guy is so damn disrespectful."

"The world is going to the dogs."

"He must have wanted to make me angry."

"I bet he thinks he's better than me."

Instead of taking these thoughts at face value, though, go into metacognition mode and look more closely at them. Keep asking questions like, *So what does that mean?* Or, *Why is that so bad?*

"That guy disrespected me."

So, what does that mean?

"It means I am basically under attack."

Why is that so bad?

"Because I have to respond, to show him he can't just do that…"

If you keep looking at your beliefs with curiosity, you may start to see how they connect with the behaviors you choose, your self-concept, and the beliefs you hold. In this example, a person with an anger problem may discover that their unhelpful thoughts push them to lash out in rage, which actually triggers other people to respond defensively and reinforces the initial belief that everyone is hostile and ready to attack.

By looking closely at these beliefs, we could replace one or two of them. For example, the next time something makes this person angry, they could pause, take a breath, and instead think, "It's actually not the end of the world if someone is a little rude to me. I don't like it, but I don't have to respond." By getting a handle on our thoughts, we can change so much.

If we rely only on gut feeling and intuition (i.e. bias and old habit), we're susceptible to unexamined irrationality. Maybe you identified with the first example and know what low self-esteem feels like, or maybe the anger story resonated more. The truth is, we are all susceptible to our own unconscious and largely irrational motivations. How metacognition can help us uncover these is the subject of the next section.

What's really motivating you? Understanding logos, pathos and ethos

What ultimately moves people to act? What makes them decide to do one thing or the other? The ABC model highlighted the role that emotions and thoughts play in determining our behavior. But that's not the only element that inspires people to act. The philosopher Aristotle outlined three main avenues through which he believed people could be persuaded: logos, pathos and ethos.

These are a little like mental models or perspectives. The fact is that even when faced with the most objective, straightforward data, people are often inspired to act only because of other (largely irrational) motivators. Advertisers understand this—they don't dwell on the practical facts of what they're selling, but appeal to their customers' emotions, their fears and even their unconscious primal drives and core beliefs.

If you understand how people (yourself included) are motivated in this way, you make yourself a more persuasive and effective speaker, but you also equip yourself to notice how these motivations play out in your own life. This could go a long way to avoiding being duped or misled, but it also stops you from blindly following your own "intuition" down misguided paths.

The first of Aristotle's categories of persuasion is ethos, or *the appeal to authority.* When a doctor in a white lab coat tells you that the medication is safe, you believe it. Ethos is about the trust and credibility that comes from professionals, experts and leaders. If you are trying to persuade someone of your argument, the idea is to share believable and valuable credentials and vouch for your experience. You do this every time you write a flattering resume to give to a potential employer in a job interview.

On the other hand, it's worth being aware if you're particularly susceptible to appeals to authority. Are you the kind of person who buys celebrity-endorsed products or votes for a candidate simply because someone you admire also votes for them? Going with the crowd or trusting an authority figure isn't necessarily a bad rubric to follow, but pay attention. You may be missing out on what's right in front of you if you succumb to appeals to authority. It's not difficult to imagine how this motivation is exploited by everyone from ad agencies to the military to the educational system.

Pathos is the *appeal to emotions*. When you speak directly to your audience's emotions, you bypass their rational thinking and connect straight to their hearts, their suffering, their lived experience, their hopes and dreams. This can be powerful stuff—but it can also massively disarm critical thinking! Many people use pathos to deliberately disarm a more rational analysis of the facts at hand. For example, a charity fundraiser may focus on heart-breaking anecdotes and sad images, knowing that this will get a better result than merely mentioning accurate but less impressive statistics.

In fact, pathos is most dangerous when it's subtle. Light touches of passion and emotion can make all the difference between factually identical outcomes or options. We've already looked in detail at the ins and outs of critically analyzing the claims people make—but someone batting their eyelashes or using warm, uplifting language may ultimately have a more profound effect on your perception of their argument.

If you're susceptible to appeals to emotion (and let's be honest, we all are), then you need to take special care to separate out the *factual* content from the *emotional* content. Be honest about your appraisals and assumptions. Are you agreeing with a claim because it's accompanied by inspiring music and cool visuals? Do you accept an argument because the person making it seems really funny and interesting? Not many of us would admit to it at first blush, but the truth is that, when examined, these little things can and do sway us heavily, if we're not paying attention.

Finally, there is logos, *the appeal to reason.* This is when we are persuaded by an argument because it appears reasonable, rational and logical. If you're wondering how this could be a bad thing, consider how easy it is to take random, objective data and use it to support patently false conclusions. Statistics are notorious when it comes to this kind of manipulation. Superficial logic, premises that seems reasonable on the surface, and plain old logical fallacies can be used to persuade you of something you'd otherwise not buy into.

For example, consider how often scientific language is used to sell bogus products or promote completely unrelated concepts. For example, "Peer-reviewed literature in journals explains garlic's antibacterial properties, therefore if you wear a bulb of garlic around your neck, you can't catch a cold," or "Scientists discuss the theoretical possibility of parallel universes, therefore you need to buy my book about learning to astral walk."

This is not logic and reason per se, but the *appeal* to it. You may be tempted to agree with the person presenting reams of charts and graphs without taking a closer look. Combine this tactic with a strong appeal to authority and a bit of pathos for good measure, and you may well find yourself persuaded to go along with something completely irrational.

To get around appeals to logic, simply refuse to immediately accept any claims, even if they're shrouded in the appearance of stone-cold fact and logic. After all, haven't some of the greatest atrocities in human history been perpetrated by those who sincerely believed that science and reason were on their side?

It's especially important to be vigilant for appeals to logic when you are not familiar with the subject at hand. In a way, the appeal to logic is also something of an appeal to pathos—the emotions often conjured by arguments of this kind are ones of calmness, certainty and even superiority. We may be attracted to certain arguments simply because they make us *feel* as though we're being very rational and logical in our approach. Countless products and services are advertised this way—the company tells its prospective customer, "Don't worry about all those silly people out there getting swayed by their emotions. *You're* smarter than that. That's why you buy XYZ—because it's the logical, intelligent choice."

If you are writing a speech or trying to persuade someone round to your point of view, it can be useful to bear these three motivations in mind—truly effective campaigns are often those that blend all three for a powerful, irresistible case. But perhaps there is more use in understanding how we ourselves are vulnerable or receptive to these appeals, so that we can recognize when we are being manipulated and influenced.

When we use Aristotle's model, we are alert not only to the factual content we encounter in the world, but the manner in which this content is presented, and ultimately the motivations of the people behind the claims. The next time you look at an ad on TV or in a magazine, listen to a politician on TV, watch a documentary about an important issue, read a paragraph in a history textbook, listen to a family member relate a complicated story, or go to church on Sunday, listen closely to what aspect the speaker is most closely addressing in their audience. It may be all three!

Takeaways

- Though it seems like a promising shortcut, intuition is not a viable replacement for critical thinking because it doesn't allow us to challenge and replace irrational beliefs and thoughts. Though we may like to think

that our intuition is an unconscious superpower we possess, it is usually influenced by our past choices and emotions, none of which are conducive to good decision-making.
- Metacognition is thinking about our own thinking. It gives us a degree of conscious control over our thoughts, feelings and behaviors that we can't attain when we are fully identified with and unconscious of our own biases, prejudices, habits and assumptions.
- We can practice metacognition by using the ABC model. We can see all the ways that an activating event can trigger us to experience certain thoughts and feelings (called beliefs), and then these instigate resulting consequences, such as behaviors or secondary emotions. By analyzing situations using the ABC framework, we can replace unhelpful or inaccurate beliefs with those that better align with our goals.
- None of us appraises factual information in a vacuum—we all are motivated to act for different reasons. Aristotle outlined appeals to reason, emotion or authority (logos, pathos and ethos) as three primary persuasive forces. We do things

either when someone in a position of authority tells us to do them, or if they appeal to our emotions by tugging at our heartstrings, or appear to make a rational argument in favor of a certain action. If we are consciously aware of when these appeals are being made to manipulate us, we can act accordingly, or else use these principles to help us become more convincing to others.

- The hardest to tackle of Aristotle's three appeals is the appeal of logic, especially because the illusion of logic also speaks to our emotions. However, when you're the one trying to motivate someone, it is best to use all three to make an especially strong case.

Chapter 5. How to think in systems

By this point in the book, you might be starting to see that the question of *how* to think is extraordinarily complex. We can inhabit a whole universe of different mental models, or blends of each, or switch between them as need dictates. We can encounter contrasting mental models and engage with them, almost changing the reality of a situation by changing the perspective through which we perceive that "reality." We even make models about the models we use (as we are doing with this very book) and use tools of critical thinking and analysis to unpick the very arguments that allowed us to establish the rules of critical thinking in the first place.

Phew! Metacognition can get complicated.

"Systems thinking" is a large, three-dimensional model capable of containing and managing all the complexity that comes with being an intelligent, conscious being trying to become aware of and master its own thinking processes. Before we dive in and discover what it means to think in terms of systems, be aware that we are discussing higher-order, necessarily abstract concepts that may seem a little vague at times. We'll try to consider a few practical examples, but the essence of systems thinking is beyond the detail.

We can see systems thinking as encompassing an entire range of attitudes and principles. A system is a larger whole composed of smaller units, each working in its own way towards the greater function of the entire system. The system is orders of magnitude more complex—we can zoom in on one element to understand it, or we can look at that element's place in the system, and gain insight by understanding its position within the whole.

Systems thinking is the mindset that allows us to perceive and work with data from a higher order of understanding. Importantly, it enables us to view ourselves in this way, even when we are embedded in systems larger and more complex than we can at first comprehend. When we can engage this mode of thinking with clarity and control, we are infinitely better equipped to make wise decisions, to navigate real-life situations on all scales, to take beneficial action, and to make meaning of our lives.

Principles of systems thinking
Let's consider some elements of systems thinking, the first of which is the ability to comprehend the *interconnectedness* of any system. Here, we shift out of seeing events around us in a linear, disconnected way, and see instead that a system is circular (or even spherical!).

It is a recognition of this principle that makes an ecologist look out and see the web of relationships that form a complex, mature rainforest. And it's a lack of understanding of this principle that gives a farmer tunnel vision when working his crops—he cannot understand how soil erosion, the pesticides he uses, the population of native owls, the average temperature last spring and the quality of his corn harvest are all intimately connected. He sees only his corn. And ignores the rest.

Modern, industrialized nations view human beings as essentially islands; we see ourselves as individuals who merely exist beside one another, who are not connected except perhaps in the capitalist transactional sense. But an expanded view sees that every element of a system is dependent on every other element.

The book or device you're holding in your hands was created by someone. They in turn depended on countless other humans, organisms, and environmental factors to do that work. The calories they burnt to do that work came from the food they ate, which emerged from a complex web of relationships extending all the way back to the sun, on which all life on earth depends.

These interconnected relationships extend not only across space but across time, and play out over physical, psychological, financial and even spiritual and emotional planes, which themselves interact. The relationships are non-linear—they mutually influence one another, and there are many, many players involved, at all scales.

A wonderful example is to imagine that any system is like a living, breathing organism; a body. Rather than the universe being a cold, dead place, it's a place wherein every part plays its role. This perspective offers an enriched, subtle view of reality as opposed to a more linear, mechanical one.

As an example, early psychological theories tended to focus on the individual. What was wrong with a specific person? What was going on in their brains, their bodies? But more sophisticated modern psychological theories are now engaging a systems mindset, and acknowledging the multidimensional influences on our behaviors, identities, and well-being (think culture, politics, socio-economic status, family, religion, gender, historical period...)

In fact, with a systems mindset, you stop seeing individual elements at all. Every node in the web merely becomes an expression of its surrounding relationships.

Synthesis is a concept closely related to interconnectedness. The definition of synthesis is simple: it's the act of combining two or more things to create something completely new. While analysis dissects data to understand it in detail, synthesis puts it all back together again to see how everything works as a whole.

It's the opposite of a "reductionistic" worldview, where the complexity of life is truncated. As we've seen, any time we make a model of the world, we necessarily *reduce* it, and lose some of its essence. Synthesis, on the other hand, is about restoring an idea to its original (often intimidatingly messy) dimension. It's holistic. We acknowledge the bigger picture while still seeing the smaller units that make it up.

Whenever we engage in synthesis, we open ourselves up to perceive interconnectedness. At the start of the book, we spoke about *how* to think rather than *what* to think. We became interested in the relationships and functions of the elements in a whole, rather than just focusing on the elements themselves—i.e. learning more facts or gaining more data.

Brilliant business ideas often come about when synthesis is employed. Maybe you look and see that market A is saturated, and so is market B. But what happens when you create a business that serves the untapped market at the *connection between A and B*? Synthesis can help us resolve conflict (what if *both* sides are right? What would that look like?) plan research (what hidden variable is influencing both my independent and dependent variable right now?) or reach a diagnosis (how is the *interaction* of these different symptoms bringing about this meta-symptom?).

You may have heard of the maxim underlying what's called Gestalt (German for "whole") thinking—i.e. that the "whole is greater than the sum of the parts" or 2+2=5. This goes some way to explaining another aspect of systems thinking: that of *emergence*. A system, essentially, is bigger than the synthesis of all its parts; this characteristic is the reason we talk about systems at all. A pile of innards lying in a dissection dish is not the same as a digestive system, and by that token a human being is much more than a collection of different biological systems. The system is its own being, beyond the identities of the individual parts.

Emergence describes this fact: that big things emerge when smaller things aggregate. It's how life itself emerged on the planet. This is not top-down organization (unless you include intelligent design) but bottom-up. Complex phenomena emerge from simple units, combined. This is why the programmers who designed the AI game-playing program Alpha Go were surprised at the way the machine ultimately thought and interacted. It learnt, it adapted, and it turned out to be an entity much larger and more complex than the components from which it was made.

Another important concept is *feedback*. When things are interconnected, feedback loops become possible. The human body regulates itself using different kinds of feedback, for example. The pituitary gland can stimulate the release of certain hormones from various glands, but when the concentration of those hormones reaches a certain level, specialized cells detect the increase and communicate with the hypothalamus, which then dials back the pituitary, essentially telling it to stimulate the glands less.

This is a self-regulating loop, because its normal function maintains balance or equilibrium. If hormone levels rise too much, the loop brings them down again. When they're too low, more is produced. This is called negative feedback—because the result of a change in a system *negates* or counters the original stimulus that set off that process.

Positive feedback is less common in the human body, but can be best illustrated when you think about the concept of an "anxiety spiral." You are anxious about something, and you noticing those anxiety symptoms actually makes you feel more stressed. So you stress more, and create more anxiety symptoms, and so on until the loop is forcibly interrupted somehow. This feedback occurs when the result of a change actually acts to enhance or amplify its own effect, and is inherently unstable.

In a system, loops are constantly balancing or amplifying one another's effects, and if we understand these relationships, we can step in to intervene or even take advantage. But of course, elements are constantly impacting one another, whether it's in a loop or not. Understanding *causality* is another aspect of systems thinking that comes from understanding interconnectedness.

Systems are dynamic and constantly changing and moving. Cause and effect are behind much of this movement. Learning to see the interplay of cause and effect enriches your perspective, allows you to identify feedback loops, illuminates connections and relationships, and helps you answer *why* questions. Actions lead to results which then shape future actions. Sounds simple, but being cognizant of the power of this principle can make a huge difference.

Finally, let's consider one final principle, *systems mapping*. This is essentially what it sounds like—creating a map of all the different elements in a system to best understand how they're connected to one another. It's only when you have a very clear picture of the system in front of you that you can start to intervene, make changes or ask further questions.

Perhaps without knowing it, you've encountered and used systems maps before, or even created your own. The diagram explaining the water cycle you were introduced to in school is a perfect example, and is meant to highlight causal relationships between "reservoirs" and the flow of water between them. Diagrams like this work well for emphasizing feedback loops or particular networks of relationships. You'll see them used to capture everything from climate models to flowcharts designed to help decision-making.

But as with any model, we need to remember that "the map is not the territory" and that we can in fact represent data in multiple ways. The only question is whether our model has the power to help us explain, understand or predict. There are no "correct" maps—only ones with greater or lesser utility, given our purpose.

We could map a system using a graph with an X and Y axis, and plot behavior or phenomenon against one another or against time. This is useful for understanding how events unfold, and can show us the details of relationship between two variables in particular. Again, the way we choose variables and how we map them is completely arbitrary.

An "iceberg model" is what we've been using in this book. If we were to draw a pyramid, we could map out the different levels of understanding: the bottom, largest level could be mental models; the next one could be mental structures like thoughts, beliefs, and values; the highest could be events or behaviors. Thus, we can fit anything into our model and emphasize how the lower levels inform and support the upper levels. For example, a "scout" mental model can sustain thoughts and beliefs such as "disagreement is not a threat," which could lead to actions like civil debate and asking questions.

Really, systems mapping is whatever you want—or need—it to be. You could draw a web of nodes connected to one another, or use a combination of those discussed here. Systems mapping is not just for formal academic or business environments. You'd be surprised how much clarity can be gained when you sit down with a pen and paper and map out your own mental models, or try to understand your thoughts with a "mind map."

As an example, a psychologist may be working with a client who is part of a large and complex family group. The psychologist might one day whip out a piece of paper and draw several circles on the page, each representing a family member, with the client as a circle in the middle. The psychologist could then ask the client to fill in some arrows between the circles, to show who influences whom, with the line's darkness indicating the intensity of the influence. Literally *seeing* this web of relationships in one diagram can be powerful—the client may suddenly realize just how much pressure and control is coming at them from all sides.

Now, we've considered several different principles behind systems thinking, but really, they are all concerned with adapting our mental models to reflect the complexity, interconnectedness and dynamism of the world we actually live in. These building blocks will allow you to make the shift in perspective that leads to more creative, divergent thinking beyond our ordinary limitations.

Systems are everywhere
Are you wondering how all of this theory can be applied to real life, out there? Though you might agree that reality is laid out as a system, it can be hard to see it in your own circumstances. So, let's try to make these principles concrete by imagining real situations where systems thinking offers an advantage when it comes

to insight, decision-making or just a worthwhile life in general.

Consider a problem like poverty. There are solutions to this problem, but the quality and effectiveness of your solution would depend on the sophistication of the mental model you used to understand it. You could decide that welfare was the answer—if people don't have money, give them some. But it doesn't take a genius to see that poverty is a persistent problem, even in areas where welfare is available.

A systems thinker can take a step back and look at poverty not as an isolated problem that is merely defined as "some people don't have money." Rather, it's an effect, of which there are many causes. If these were diagrammed in a systems map, it would a complex web of influences, including things like education and discrimination.

Here, a systems thinker might notice not only that things are interconnected, but that there are positive feedback loops—the more education, the better the employment prospects, the lower the chance of poverty. This systems thinking allows us to see that a longer-term solution would also focus on improving access to education and better jobs.

To take a look at what is essentially the same problem through a different lens, consider a married couple who is fighting about housework. The wife is angry that the husband doesn't do his share. But this is only the surface event. Imagine an iceberg model where the argument about housework is the "tip of the iceberg." Just beneath that we can start to ask what has been happening up till then, what the trends are, and what changes have brought about the current situation.

We might find that the woman has recently begun working when previously she was a stay-at-home mother. Accustomed to his wife doing everything at home, the husband is now unwilling to do more housework himself, even though they now work equal hours. But what's beneath *this*? What is it about the system that has affected not just the husband and wife, but their relationship? Perhaps we learn that the rising cost of living, and a reduction in work hours for the husband due to massive shifts in his industry, have meant that the wife needs to work for the family to survive.

But what's beneath this? Digging even deeper, we see a bedrock of mental models informing the couple's assumptions, beliefs and values. The husband believes a man should never do housework, whether his wife works or not. In this case, his beliefs are a microcosm of the bigger cultural and political system they both live in. So, it is not really a problem about housework at all.

Let's imagine this couple have been fighting for ages and are now in couples' therapy, trying to decide whether it's worth saving their marriage. They have some big decisions to make. During their sessions, the therapist uses systems thinking to help them identify how, as a family, their values, beliefs, actions and needs are all influencing one another's.

Perhaps they begin to see how different one another's mental models are, and how their arguments always seem to go nowhere because they don't actually share the same set of values or underlying assumptions. The husband approaches the issue with a soldier mindset, thinking like an engineer, while the wife is a scout who is working from the mindset of a diplomat or peacekeeper. By carefully considering the "bigger picture," they both become empowered to make informed decisions about how they want to move forward.

All three of these examples may seem unconnected on the surface, but you can probably see that each in themselves is a smaller reflection of a much bigger phenomenon that connects them all— poverty and its effects on human lives. It's systems thinking that allows people to see how everything slots together; how the political influences the personal, how the past is part of the present, and how unrelated events and people are actually intimately connected to one another, if only we can take a broad enough view to see how.

Questions to ask to activate a system mindset

- What mental model am I using right now? How has this influenced my framing of the problem and the way I ask questions?
- What else has influenced my current situation? Think of people, ideas and events that have had an impact.
- Instead of looking at the people or events in question, can I look instead at the *connections* between them, i.e. their relationships? How does this change how I view things?
- What is my scope of action? What is my relationship to other elements in this system, and how can I affect them?
- Can I visualize the system I am embedded within? Can I visualize it differently, and does this change anything?
- What am I missing here? What perspective could I adopt that would allow me to see a different side of this situation?
- How will my own choices affect others, and how will that in turn come back to impact me?
- In the broadest sense possible, what caused my current situation or problem?

- Is the way I'm understanding my role in the system accurate? Is there some other approach that would serve me better?
- How would my situation look from a completely different point of view, i.e. from the perspective of another person in my system?
- Can I zoom way out and look at this problem after a year or ten years have passed? How does it look when I zoom way in and examine each tiny detail?
- Can I represent my understanding of the situation using a diagram? How else can I display this data?

Takeaways

- A systems thinking mindset appreciates the complexity and depth of reality itself. It's a higher-order, three-dimensional, dynamic perspective that seeks a broader view on ordinary events.
- The main principle of systems thinking is interconnectedness, i.e. the idea that smaller components arrange themselves in bigger networks or webs. Acknowledging this allows us greater insight and understanding. When we realize that everything within a certain

system is interconnected, it allows us to broaden the horizons of our thinking and also tackle problems more effectively, since we no longer see things in isolation.
- Other principles include synthesis (two things can be combined to create a third, different thing), and emergence (bigger things can arise from the combination of smaller units; the whole is greater than the sum of the parts). Synthesis is an antidote to the reductionism that is a common explanatory toll in our time. When we synthesize, we connect one thing with the other and see how particular links between a few parts affect the whole. Similarly, emergence tells us that small things can aggregate to form one huge thing, an insight that is often overlooked when analyzing specific systems.
- Feedback occurs in systems, either positive (amplifying) or negative (balancing); understanding these cause and effect relationships enhances our understanding and problem-solving capacity.
- We can map/diagram systems according to our needs and perspectives. We can

have a system for our workflow, our routine, or for when we tackle specific issues that recur in our lives. By engaging in systems-based thinking, we make our lives more efficient and easy because we've done the hard part of thinking our actions through. We can also use systems-inspired questions to help us see beyond our limited perspectives.

Chapter 6. How to think with induction and deduction

What we ultimately want to do whenever we "reason" is to arrive at some kind of conclusion we can trust. What distinguishes robust, logical, evidence-based thought from mere opinion or claim is how the information is structured and presented. We can arrive at a conclusion via different paths; on these paths we lay down stepping-stones—premises—and if they are sufficient, we'll arrive at our conclusion.

Two main paths of reasoning are deductive and inductive reasoning, the focus of this chapter. You probably use both kinds without even knowing you do, or even a mix of both. But as with all mental models and tools, they become infinitely more valuable when used with conscious intention.

Deductive reasoning, to put it very simply, "moves from the general to the specific." This is where we take broad, general ideas and concepts and from them, try to say something true about a more specific situation. A common example goes as follows:

Premise 1: All men are philosophers

Premise 2: Socrates is a man

Conclusion: Socrates is a philosopher

Premise 1 is a general idea that, when combined with the more specific premise 2, allows us to reach the conclusion. In this example, as long as we know both the premises are true, the conclusion *must* be true. In other words, the premises here *prove* the conclusion, not simply offer evidence or support for it. The validity of the argument (i.e. whether the conclusion logically follows) is, however, unaffected by the truth of the premises. You can have a logical argument that nevertheless has untrue premises and conclusion, for example:

Premise 1: All men are toasters

Premise 2: Mariah Carey is a man

Conclusion: Mariah Carey is a toaster

What this tells us is that an important part of an argument is its *structure*, and not the specific details of its premises.

In real life, science uses deductive reasoning all the time. For example, if every animal so far discovered with wings and a beak also lays eggs, you might predict that the new animal you've discovered with wings and beak will also lay eggs. Any time you use facts, rules, or general principles to arrive at a specific conclusion about a novel situation in front of you, you've accomplished deductive reasoning.

As you can imagine, though, the weakness of this sort of argument rests in the premises—the argument is useless if the general premises you've identified are not in fact true. You need to start with 100 percent true facts—something that's quite difficult to do in real life!

Luckily, this is not the only kind of reasoning we have at our disposal. Inductive reasoning goes the opposite direction—it moves from the specific to the general. In other words, the argument considers a few specific observations or premises and attempts to construct a general rule or pattern from them.

Here, the conclusion is never 100 percent *proven* by the premises. Rather, the premises support the conclusion in the same way as legs support a table. The stronger and more numerous the legs of the table, the more solid the table, i.e. the more we can trust the final conclusion. It's a question of doing what we can to find the *probable* or most likely conclusion that fits our premises.

As an example, imagine you eat peanut butter one day and then you feel sick. You eat it again the next day and you feel sick again. In fact, every time you eat peanut butter, you notice the same symptoms. You also notice that when you don't eat peanut butter, you don't experience the symptoms. This is an inductive argument that might end with the conclusion: peanut butter makes you sick.

Of course, this is your best guess. It might be possible that chance events or some other unknown cause is interfering, and peanut butter is in fact harmless. But with every additional observation, you may have relative faith in the *probability* of your conclusion—i.e., it's the best way to explain your premises.

A big difference between deductive and inductive reasoning is how they're used, and what type of knowledge they help generate. Inductive arguments are most used to predict what will happen in the future: If I eat peanut butter, what will happen? Deductive arguments are employed more to prove a conclusion. Deductive arguments prove their conclusion 100 percent, but inductive arguments can possess greater or lesser strength, depending on the quality of their premises. If you use a deductive argument correctly, your conclusion will always be valid... but it won't necessarily be true.

Let's look closer: Arguments can possess both *validity* and *soundness*. Validity is in the structure—an argument is valid if it's impossible for the premises to be true but the conclusion false. It's a question of logic. A valid argument is the one about Socrates above. An invalid argument is:

Premise 1: If I drink at work, the boss will fire me.

Premise 2: The boss fired me.

Conclusion: I drank at work.

You can see in the above that it is in fact possible for the premises to be true and the conclusion false, i.e. the boss fired you for some other reason. In fact, in the above example, both premises can be true and *even the conclusion can be true* while the argument itself is still invalid!

Soundness takes things a step further: a sound argument is where all the premises are true *and* the argument is valid. To really get a handle on arguments, we need to understand the difference between true, valid and sound. Many people get tripped up in complex debates because real-life arguments are messy—they're a combination of deductive and indictive, there are many premises (some of them irrelevant), some premises may be true but used in a fundamentally invalid argument, and so on.

However, as long as we can slow down, understand the premises, the conclusion and the underlying structure in front of us, we can make reasonable and informed decisions.

We can use deductive reasoning in any situation where we begin with a handful of known-to-be-true facts or premises. Whether it's in piecing together a murder prosecution case, interpreting test results, problem solving in the workplace, or trying to make sense of a complicated logistical problem, deductive reasoning can help us reach a conclusion we know is sound. Deductive reasoning covers all the "if/then" style problems we encounter in a complex world—but it requires us to genuinely remove emotion, assumption, and bias, and work only with the facts.

If we don't really have "facts" to deal with, then inductive reasoning may work better. When we are faced with a messy situation and need to pull out a thread of cause and effect, inductive reasoning can help us organize disparate events to find one or two conclusions that explain what we see.

A scientist may be curious about a biological phenomenon, and simply gather observations at first. Then, using inductive reasoning, she can piece together a hypothesis that she tests with an experiment. She can then use deductive reasoning to construct an argument and arrive at a scientifically supported conclusion. This shows that deductive and inductive reasoning often work together (not to mention other reasoning types we haven't covered here). Let's explore deductive and inductive forms of reasoning in a little detail.

Inductive reasoning
You've probably seen it happen in a book or on TV—a super-detective like Sherlock

Holmes arriving at a scene and then immediately knowing what happened just by looking at the area. A cascade of scenes flash through his mind, telling a story of the series of events that must've happened that led to the specific arrangement and state of things in the area. He has taken a wide range of observations and immediately formed the story that led to them all. How'd he do it?

The answer is by inductive reasoning. Though the famous novels frequently call what Holmes does "deduction," this is just a common misconception. Remember, inductive reasoning goes from the specific to the general. Holmes typically made a range of specific observations (for example, the Baroness wears a size four shoe, the footprints in the snow are a size four, the Baroness had blood under her fingernails and was witnessed at the scene ten minutes after the murder was committed...) and uses these to arrive at a probable conclusion that explains them all (i.e. the Baroness is the murderer).

Sherlock Holmes famously claimed, "Once you've ruled out the impossible, whatever remains, no matter how improbable, must be true." You might recognize *this* as pure deductive reasoning, and evidence that Sherlock likely used both kinds of thinking to solve his mysteries. Holmes may use inductive reasoning to arrive at some conclusions about theory A, B and C, but then he can employ the following deductive argument:

Premise 1: There are only two kinds of events, possible and impossible.

Premise 2: There are three competing theories to explain a phenomenon, A, B and C.

Premise 3: Theory A and B are impossible.

Conclusion: Theory C is therefore the only possibility.

Now, while the way Sherlock Holmes goes about inductive reasoning makes the whole thing seem more like a superpower than a human faculty, inductive reasoning is something you're capable of as well. In fact, you do it on a daily basis.

Say you arrive home and find a puddle of water on the kitchen floor. From that piece of information, you try to backtrack to what must've happened that caused that puddle to be there. You note location (e.g., is it near the sink or underneath a leaky roof area?), amount and quality of the water (e.g., does it look like clean drinking water, or does it have a murky quality?), and surrounding objects (e.g., are there broken shards of drinking glass nearby or perhaps a toppled fishbowl?).

You then use such information to reason backward from the effect you're seeing (i.e., the puddle of water), to the most probable cause based on the details you observe (i.e., someone knocked over a drinking glass). You've just performed deduction. You've asked yourself: what conclusion best explains all these separate observations? You are doing "bottom-up" processing of the data.

Induction is essentially *reverse storytelling*. It's the art of taking the information available to you at a given moment and then reasoning backward from effect to cause.

Inductive reasoning is thus an essential skill to master when it comes to problem-solving. Induction allows you to make reasonable assumptions about the causes of events and thus enables you to solve problems at their roots.

Would you really get someone to look for and patch holes in your roof when you've studied the situation and figured out that the true cause for that puddle was a dropped drinking glass and not a leaky roof?

If you want to hone your powers of induction, there are a number of techniques you can practice. The following section outlines five of the best ways you can go about it: (1) make a fishbone diagram, (2) practice coming up with potential causes for details you observe, (3) watch people and deduce the conversations they're having, (4) talk out loud, and (5) put aside your ego to become more open-minded.

Each of these techniques will help you make sense of all the information you've gathered through the strategies of observation discussed in the previous section. In the process of becoming a master problem-solver, you need to be able to not only observe keenly, but also make sense of those observations sensibly.

Make a fishbone diagram. A fishbone diagram is a method that allows you to identify multiple potential causes for a problem or an effect. Being able to infer causes based on an observed effect is an integral aspect of induction, especially when it comes to problem-solving. Fleshing out a list of all the possible causes of a problem simultaneously provides you with a blueprint of the specific factors you need to focus on to ultimately find viable solutions.

The fishbone diagram is so structured that those causes are placed in categories, so you get a more orderly perspective of the entire situation. It's a more organized way of working in reverse from effect to cause, and is a frequently used tool for structuring brainstorming sessions. The end product is a visual display of all the factors—both from a micro and a macro perspective—

that play a role in leading to the effect or the problem.

To make a fishbone diagram, first write a problem statement or effect somewhere in the middle right portion of a whiteboard or any writing surface you've chosen. Draw a box around it, then a horizontal line across the page that ends in that problem box. That box will serve as the "head" of the fishbone.

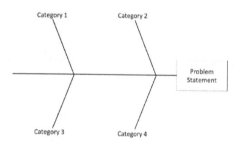

Next, draw the "bones" of the body by sketching widely spaced vertical lines that extend out of the main horizontal line. Draw bones above and below the main line, slightly slanting away from the head of the fishbone. These bones will be labeled with the different categories of the causes you come up with. It's up to you to name the categories that apply to the problem you're working on.

Every time you come up with a possible cause for the problem, write it down as a connection to the particular "bone" it's categorized under. You can write the same cause under multiple categories if applicable. Then, for each noted cause, continue asking what might've caused it, and write it down as a connection to that cause, and so on until you can no longer think of a more primary cause. This will allow you to exercise your deductive reasoning skills until you arrive at the most fundamental root causes of the problem.

When you're done with the diagram, scrutinize the causes you've listed and consider the evidence regarding them. How much does each identified cause really contribute to creating the effect? Is its link with the problem well-established and significant enough to consider seriously? Get into the habit of thinking, "What would make this cause a true and significant factor in the problem at hand?"

For example, say you're a hotel manager trying to understand the reasons behind low customer satisfaction ratings for your hotel service. Write the problem in a box as the fishbone "head" and the categories of possible causes (in this case, the four P's of service industries) as the main "bones." Doing this, the initial stages of your fishbone diagram would look like so:

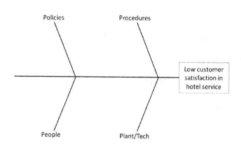

Then start filling in each category with possible causes. For example, you've identified that possible causes for the problem are (1) the slow resolution of customer complaints and (2) the hotel staff's inability to be sensitive to the customers' needs, thus leading the customer to be dissatisfied with the service.

Asking yourself why your staff may lack sensitivity to customer needs, you may consider that they work such long hours that they are reduced to providing just the bare minimum of service; they no longer have enough energy to pay more attention to customers' more specific needs. Given that, your fishbone diagram would now indicate the following:

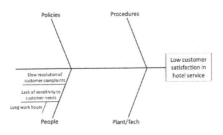

Continuing the process of asking yourself why the problem exists, you start identifying more possible causes and noting them under the given categories, leading your diagram to look something like this:

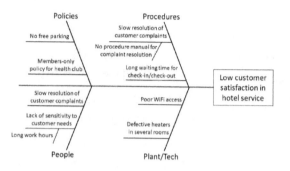

By systematically working backward from the problem to the causes, you get to identify specific aspects of your situation that you can then address accordingly. The fishbone diagram is a tool that effectively focuses your efforts to solve the problem at its roots—or, in this case, at its bones.

It's a great way to guide your thinking in the process of reverse storytelling, as it allows you to concretely trace how the problem is linked back to specific causative factors. Think of the fishbone diagram as a scaffold that helps you build up your deductive reasoning and problem-solving skills more effectively.

Note details and potential causes. Remember how one technique to sharpen your observation skills involves watching a person or a scene and noting ten details about it? You can do a "level-up" of this technique in order to develop your inductive reasoning. This exercise involves taking a scene, a person, or any other thing, and observing ten details about it. Then, for each of those details, write down five possible causes that may have led that particular detail to be the way it is. Try to vary the potential reasons you list, ranging from the plainly realistic to the downright bizarre. This will train your ability to create a story around every detail, thus exercising your skills in reverse storytelling, which is what deductive reasoning is all about.

Say you've decided to observe your neighborhood park. You note several details about it: five benches, three joggers circling the area, two kids on the seesaw, a child enjoying an ice cream cone, a man sweeping dead leaves from under a tree, a broken swing, a lunch basket abandoned by a bench, a sign supposed to say "park" but missing the letter P, a woman reading under a shade, and a large tree branch lying in the middle of a footpath.

You then take one of those details—for instance, the large tree branch on the footpath—and try to come up with five backstories explaining why the branch is there. One, the branch may have simply fallen off a tree because a huge gust of wind had knocked it off. Two, the branch may have been infected by insects and was thus hacked off by park caretakers to save the tree. Three, it may have fallen off a load of branches someone was transporting on the way to a bonfire.

Four, a group of mischievous kids may have purposefully dragged the branch to the middle of the path to trip people passing through. And five, the branch may have been placed there by a secret agent as a coded message to signify a meeting place. By trying to determine the possible causes of what you're seeing, from the mundane to the wildly creative, you're exercising your deductive powers.

Practice people-watching to induce conversation content. This is another upgraded exercise from your observation-sharpening set of techniques. When you observe people, select those engaged in a conversation you can't hear, then guess what they might be talking about. What might be the relationship between those people? What is each of them saying, and what is the other's response? What might be the motivations behind their words?

An interesting way to do this is to use book or TV characters. Witnessing a particular action or decision a character has made, try to deduce what might've led them to act or decide the way they did. Alternatively, you may watch a sitcom on mute or watch a foreign movie without subtitles. Figure out what the characters are saying to each other and state your reasons for your assumptions. You may also try to come up with two opposing stories for each scenario, then pick the story that's more likely to be true. Explain why the story you've chosen is the more sensible one, using evidence you've observed in the scene.

Say you watch a scene in which a woman is talking to a fruit vendor stationed in a food stall by the street. The woman is holding some dollar bills, while the vendor appears to be picking out fruits to offer the woman. They talk a bit more, and then the woman gives the bills to the vendor but refuses to take the fruits in exchange. The vendor smiles as the woman walks away.

What might they have said to each other during that interaction? Why did the woman give the vendor money without taking the fruits? From those questions, you could then infer a number of stories. Maybe the woman was doing an act of charity. Or maybe the woman personally knew the vendor and was paying off a debt. Or maybe they agreed that the woman would just pick up the fruits later, after she's done with an errand. Running through such stories in your head will train your mind to get into the habit of deduction.

Talk out loud. When you're trying to solve problems, it's natural that you engage in a process of thinking. But during this process, do you also have moments when you're thinking about the way you're thinking? The act of thinking about your own thinking is known as metacognition.

In recent years, problem-solving has come to be considered in light of metacognition, and for good reason—metacognition allows you to detect errors in your own deductive problem-solving methods and continually check yourself for faulty reasoning so that you avoid making errors in judgment. Enhancing your metacognitive skills is thus a powerful way to sharpen your powers of deduction and problem-solving.

So how do you boost your metacognition? The experts recommend this technique: talk out loud. The effectiveness of this method for improving problem-solving is backed by a study published by the University of Arkansas in 2011. The study looked closely into a teaching/learning strategy known as Talking Aloud Partner Problem-Solving (TAPPS), in which two people are partnered: one is tasked to solve a problem (i.e., the problem-solver), while the other (i.e., the monitor) is instructed to just listen, refrain from giving advice, and monitor the comments of the problem-solver while encouraging him to notice his own thinking pattern.

The researchers found that what actually improved the problem-solving process wasn't the monitor, but the problem-solver's own act of thinking aloud. By talking out loud, the problem-solver engages in metacognition. He's forced to put his line of reasoning in words and hear them too, thus allowing him to detect the lack of logical connections or insufficient evidence for certain assumptions. Thus, if you want to sharpen your own skills in deduction and problem-solving, you need to practice thinking out loud, whether with a partner or just by yourself.

Say you need to figure out how to increase the low number of attendees who've signed up for an upcoming seminar you've organized for start-up entrepreneurs. Talking aloud to yourself, you may say:

"Why aren't there more people signing up to attend this seminar? Maybe they're just not interested in the topic. But this topic is relevant and would surely be helpful for those who're currently involved in or even just planning to enter start-up entrepreneurship. If it's relevant and helpful, then the problem isn't the topic. Maybe info about this seminar has just failed to reach the people who would consider it relevant and helpful. So one way to attract more attendees would be to develop a more targeted marketing campaign. I should come up with a list of all start-up businesses in the area and reach out to them specifically and talk to them about this seminar. Posting info about this on social media sites for entrepreneurs might also help."

Put your ego aside. While it's tempting to think that the ability for inductive reasoning relies mainly on intellect—having the cognitive capacity to use logic in order to arrive at a fairly certain conclusion—it's important to recognize that this type of reasoning also calls for certain noncognitive skills: personal qualities and attitudes that have less to do with smarts and more to do with character. One of the most basic attitudes essential to developing a keen sense of reasoning is humility.

Humility involves having the capacity to put your ego aside and avoid a self-important perspective. In connection with inductive reasoning, it involves the willingness to backtrack on your initial assumptions, reconsider them with an open mind, and, if the situation calls for it, admit you were wrong. Only with humility can you look at the information and evidence in front of you with honesty and clarity, free from your own personal biases that tend to distort such information to cater to selfish needs.

Having too big an ego will only lead you to force the facts to fit whatever theory you've originally made up in your mind, because lack of humility can compel you to do whatever it takes to avoid showing any shortcoming on your part. An inflated ego can get in the way of seeing the facts as they are and allowing them to shape and reshape the theory, and not the other way around. Oftentimes, we want a specific outcome and will interpret all the evidence to support that outcome. Ego does not promote effective problem-solving.

Humility is thus what offers you the flexibility to respond to the evidence you discover in a way that does not distort the assumptions you end up making. Interestingly, the subjugation of women throughout history has shaped this quality in them more effectively. In general, women needed to have the capacity to accommodate others as well as be flexible enough to adjust to the situation in order to avoid or pacify conflict. The masculine way, on the other hand, valued power and dominance over flexibility and adaptation.

Confronted with something that goes against their beliefs and assumptions, the masculine way of responding is one of either defensiveness or aggression instead of accommodation. Seeking others' wisdom and taking critical feedback are considered signs of weakness and are thus avoided by masculine personalities with strong egos. Humble people, on the other hand, are more readily receptive to new information and evidence, even if it counters their initial assumptions. This grants them the ability to make decisions based on actual data and arrive at conclusions truly derived from the evidence at hand.

Take for instance Jerry, an entrepreneur who runs an online clothing store. He's run into a problem—an angry rant from an unsatisfied customer has gone viral online. His ego hurt, Jerry reacts impulsively and posts an angry reply to the customer. The whole thing blows up and Jerry starts receiving cancellations for orders left and right.

Fearing the disintegration of his business, Jerry tries to calm down and investigate the situation more closely. Upon humbly reaching out to the customer and finding her complaints well-founded, Jerry apologizes and promptly sends in a product replacement with a freebie to boot. Satisfied with the resolution, the customer posts a public appreciation of how Jerry's store effectively handled her complaint. By setting aside his ego, Jerry was able to correct his assumptions and target the cause of the problem, leading to its eventual resolution.

As another example, say you belong to one of three groups each given a hula hoop. There's a big pile of about thirty plastic balls in your midst. The challenge is to put all thirty balls within your group's own hula hoop. If everyone simply lets their ego take charge, all three groups would fight over getting the balls for themselves and make it unlikely for any single group to succeed.

But setting your ego aside will allow you to reconsider the situation and use your reason with better clarity. Why not have all three hula hoops encircle the pile of thirty balls? That way, all groups accomplish the goal. The resolution was made possible only by allowing your clarity of reason to transcend the selfish need to be the only "winner."

So there you have it—all the techniques, tips, and tricks you need to master the art of using observation and inductive reasoning toward effective problem-solving. We need to remember the key limitation behind inductive reasoning – that it only allows us to talk in *probabilities*, not in absolute truths. We can build strong arguments, but we need to be open to the possibility that we've missed a crucial detail, or allowed bias or assumption to creep in. When using inductive reasoning, the conclusion we arrive at must always come with a caveat: it is a *provisional* truth, not an absolute one.

Observation, when done correctly, allows you to gather every bit of information you need to know in order to solve a problem. You can improve your observation skills by becoming more detail-oriented, devoting 100 percent of your focus, being alert to deviations from the baseline, having insight into people's self-perceptions, and seeing how the details fit into the big picture.

Inductive reasoning is what turns the information you gathered from observation into significant assumptions, conclusions, and judgments. By becoming proficient at this kind of thinking, you get to use the evidence in front of you as breadcrumbs that lead to the root causes of a problem, which you can then address more effectively. Using the fishbone diagram, enumerating potential causes of every detail you observe, practicing people-watching to deduce conversations, talking through problem-solving out loud, and putting aside your ego to be more open-minded are all essential techniques to help you achieve expert-level inductive reasoning.

Deductive reasoning
What about deductive reasoning, then?

As you might have guessed, pure deductive reasoning is not all that common in real life. As you may recall, deductive reasoning moves from the general to the specific. In the scientific method, whenever we use an established theory to make predictions and statements about a set of specific observations, we are using deduction. But we need those well-established theories and facts to start with!

A very common form of deductive reasoning is what's called a syllogism. This is where two statements—a minor and a major premise—can be used to arrive at a conclusion. For example:

Major premise: All life forms are carbon-based.

Minor premise: This is a life form.

Conclusion: It must be carbon-based.

As you can see, the broader theory is used to make statements about the smaller observation. The above is a "categorical" syllogism—i.e. we make conclusions based on how we categorize and define things. A "conditional" syllogism takes the "if/then" format, for example:

Major premise: If I don't pass this class, I'll fail the term.

Minor premise: I didn't pass this class.

Conclusion: I'm going to fail the term.

In this example too, the general is used to make a specific claim—in this case a prediction. The deductive argument we saw Sherlock Holmes using ("if we eliminate the impossible, what remains is the truth") is called a "disjunctive" syllogism, and is in an either/or format, for example:

Major premise: Mammals are either male or female.

Minor premise: This mammal is not male.

Conclusion: This mammal is female.

Note here that, unlike with inductive arguments, the conclusion is *100 percent true*, if the major premises are. Deductive arguments lead to their conclusions with the same certainty as algebraic equations. Nevertheless, we can still make mistakes when using deductive reasoning. Look at the following example:

Major premise: All swans are white.

Minor premise: That bird over there is white.

Conclusion: That bird over there is a swan.

Can you see the problem? Both premises are correct, but the conclusion could very well be incorrect, i.e. that the bird over there is some other white bird, and not a swan. **Generally, the weakness in inductive arguments comes down to the quality of the premises themselves. But with a deductive argument, errors can also come down to the structure**. If you believe you are looking at a deductive argument, appraise it as you would a mathematical expression. Your premise and conclusion need to fit together as neatly and logically as the argument "If x=1 and y=2, then 2x+y=4."

The problem with the swan argument is that there is a hidden assumption that is not true, i.e. that *only* swans are white. If we are aware that we're including this assumption in the argument, we can examine it to see if it's true (it's not) and remove it to improve our argument. If we barge ahead without carefully considering our assumptions and foregone conclusions, we have actually entered the realm of induction without realizing it.

Despite the flaws of deductive reasoning, it is generally a more airtight and reliable method of argumentation. This makes it more conducive to discussions, debates, and general conversation. If you're looking to make an argument, framing it in a syllogism will always make it appear more accurate, whereas inductive arguments can end up sounding like broad generalizations.

However, each has their own place; we simply need to know how best to use them depending on the circumstances.

Takeaways

- Two fundamental paths to arriving at an argument's conclusion include inductive and deductive reasoning. These are also known as merely probable and airtight forms of reasoning based on how valid the conclusions derived from them are.
- Deductive reasoning uses a general principle (such as a theory or known fact) to say something about a specific observation, whereas induction works the other way, trying to establish a general conclusion that can explain the specific observations or given premises.
- Arguments possess both validity and soundness—validity is concerned with the internal logic of an argument, but an argument is only sound if the argument is logical *and* the premises are true. Thus, an argument can be formally valid, i.e. structured in a valid form, but that doesn't mean it is sound or that it actually holds true. For that, we need to assess the truth value of the premises.

- We can use inductive reasoning to help us fine-tune our powers of observation and "reverse storytelling" to construct probable causes from observations. Inductive arguments always move from specific bits of information which are then used to arrive at a general conclusion. We can use deductive reasoning whenever we are working with known facts or given theories to help us understand new data. It is best employed when we know that the premises of our theories are factually accurate, so as to arrive at true conclusions.
- The fishbone diagram is a good tool to map out inductive arguments. Start by drawing a line through the middle and stating your conclusion at the right end. Along the line, draw diagonal arrows with causes behind that conclusion. Use your deductive skills to further elaborate on your causes and state the reasons behind them as well.
- Both deductive and indictive reasoning have their place—it's up to us to use them wisely and appropriately, according to the situation at hand.

Summary Guide

INTRODUCTION

- One of the most common mistakes humans make is that we confuse knowledge with the ability to think. Human beings possess both crystallized and fluid intelligence, i.e. banked knowledge vs. a method or process for learning and engaging with new information. While the former is useful in certain specific situations, the latter can be employed as a general tool for tackling problems.
- The aim of this book is to help readers think about their thinking or fluid intelligence. The way we think is generally influenced by a conscious or unconscious model in our minds. This model shapes our experience and perception of everything around us. By becoming aware of the model

we follow, we can improve it to include more critical thinking, curiosity, clarity of thought, etc.
- We can increase our metacognition (thinking about thinking) by understanding that mental models are tools we can use with conscious intention. They are like blueprints that help us think about different situations and problems in appropriate ways without spending too much time analyzing them from scratch.
- Mental models shape our entire lived experience, so by changing our mental models, we can also change our habits, our attitudes, our perceptions, and more. Often, we adopt narrow models that are actively harmful for us because of how they distort or exclude reality. Having the right model can give you an altogether new framework for creating meaning and imagining the possibilities in everything life throws at you.
- Metacognition of this kind improves every area of life, helping us to learn, adapt, evolve, and engage with the

world in intelligent, dynamic ways. You need not know much about the specifics of the situation (for example, about coffee machines if you're trying to fix one), but if you have a good model for fixing machines in general, you can tackle a wider range of issues.

CHAPTER 1. HOW TO BE CLEAR-MINDED

- Every single person is susceptible to falling prey to old, outdated thinking habits, biases, cognitive distortions, etc. Experts in particular, for all their knowledge, are notorious for being unable to escape their preconceived notions and rigid thinking because they have become accustomed to applying the same models over and over. To rid ourselves of this issue, we must learn how to be more clear-minded.
- Being clear-minded means seeing reality without the distortion of our bias, expectations, prejudices, assumptions, unconscious drives or cognitive errors. Contrary to what we

think, our orientation to reality is never neutral. The mindset we hold, consciously or unconsciously, influences our perception, and the content and quality of our thoughts.
- There are two fundamental orientations to the unknown: approach or defend. The scout or growth mindset adopts the former strategy and embraces the new with curiosity and humility; the soldier or fixed mindset encounters the unknown intending only to defend already-held beliefs. We can embrace a scout mindset by remembering that being wrong is not a flaw or weakness, but a necessary part of learning.
- Too often, we attempt to confirm and reinforce things we already believe to be true. However, the key to being clear-headed is actually the exact opposite: actively seeking things that go against what we think. Darwin's golden rule is to deliberately entertain information that conflicts with deeply held beliefs, so as to guard against intellectual blind spots.

- The primary factor that prevents us from being open to thoughts, opinions, or facts contrary to our beliefs is our armored ego. An armored ego is a threat to learning and understanding. It is the need we feel to justify away mistakes, erroneous modes of thinking, etc., instead of taking steps to acknowledge these mistakes and improve on them. We need to become aware of unconscious defense mechanisms so we can remove them and see with more clarity.

CHAPTER 2. HOW TO ACCURATELY SEE REALITY

- It's not enough to remove obstacles to our clear thinking; we also need to make sure that the way we appraise reality is actually accurate. A mental model is a representation of reality, but the "map is not the territory" and we need to remember that models are necessarily simplified. We need to consistently examine our model's limitations and assumptions by asking ourselves

questions and following Darwin's golden rule. Once we find that our model is incomplete, we must take active steps to stop using the same mode of thinking.
- Thought experiments are a useful tool for thinking about our beliefs, assumptions, and various hypotheses we come up with while tackling routine issues in our lives. They can help us hypothetically test out our assumptions, and follow through on hypotheses set by our models. The way we do this is by taking our beliefs and assumptions to their logical conclusion and critically examining everything that is implied or follows from the line of thought we considered in our experiment.
- There are two levels of thinking, first and second-order thinking. First-order thinking is largely superficial and seeks to resolve or answer any question/issue we face based on our intuitive leanings. Second-order thinking entails seeing consequences and possibilities beyond the immediate present, especially during decision-making. In the former, the goal is simply to make a choice, whereas in the latter it is to make an informed, well-thought-out one.

- Different perspectives and worldviews are tools to help us achieve our goals. We can adopt the mindset of an artist, scientist, psychologist, designer, etc. to help us access different aspects of reality—each has its virtues when used consciously.

CHAPTER 3. HOW TO THINK CRITICALLY AND DETERMINE TRUTH

- Thinking critically is the step-by-step process by which we process new data to arrive at well-supported conclusions—or else critically appraise the claims of others. By mastering this skill, we learn how to come up with compelling arguments and build coherent, well-informed worldviews that are not full of biases and rigid thinking. It also helps us analyze the wealth of information we come across on a daily basis. A lot of what we read on the news, for example, is opinion disguised as fact, and critical thinking will help you segregate the two thoroughly.

- The Toulmin method is a way to formally identify your argument's claim, grounds, warrant, backing, qualifier and rebuttal. The claim is essentially your conclusion, the grounds are premises for the conclusion, warrant is an explanation of how and why the premises lead to the conclusion, while backing is proof that the premises are actually true. Qualifiers are any clarifications that need to be made, while rebuttals are answers to counterarguments.
- Assumptions are the biggest threat to critical thinking. We need to identify both descriptive and value judgments in our own and others' arguments so as not to be led astray. Value judgements are hard to reconcile because you can't really argue with someone who has a fundamentally different view of the world. However, descriptive judgements are essentially unqualified assumptions that, when questioned, make the argument fall apart.
- Critical thinking can be used to assess our own thought processes and help us arrive at better decisions if we take the time to unpack our supporting

arguments. If you have a certain belief, break it down into premises and conclusion, or the main claim and everything that supports it in your view. Think which premise is the weakest and consider whether it can be strengthened through proof or better analysis. If it cannot be, you have a belief that rests on weak arguments, in which case you should discard it and adopt a more rational outlook.

CHAPTER 4. HOW TO THINK ABOUT YOUR THINKING

- Though it seems like a promising shortcut, intuition is not a viable replacement for critical thinking because it doesn't allow us to challenge and replace irrational beliefs and thoughts. Though we may like to think that our intuition is an unconscious superpower we possess, it is usually influenced by our past choices and emotions, none of which are conducive to good decision-making.
- Metacognition is thinking about our own thinking. It gives us a degree of

conscious control over our thoughts, feelings and behaviors that we can't attain when we are fully identified with and unconscious of our own biases, prejudices, habits and assumptions.
- We can practice metacognition by using the ABC model. We can see all the ways that an activating event can trigger us to experience certain thoughts and feelings (called beliefs), and then these instigate resulting consequences, such as behaviors or secondary emotions. By analyzing situations using the ABC framework, we can replace unhelpful or inaccurate beliefs with those that better align with our goals.
- None of us appraises factual information in a vacuum—we all are motivated to act for different reasons. Aristotle outlined appeals to reason, emotion or authority (logos, pathos and ethos) as three primary persuasive forces. We do things either when someone in a position of authority tells us to do them, or if they appeal to our emotions by tugging at our heartstrings, or appear to make a rational argument in favor of a certain action. If we are consciously aware of when these appeals are being made to

manipulate us, we can act accordingly, or else use these principles to help us become more convincing to others.
- The hardest to tackle of Aristotle's three appeals is the appeal of logic, especially because the illusion of logic also speaks to our emotions. However, when you're the one trying to motivate someone, it is best to use all three to make an especially strong case.

CHAPTER 5. HOW TO THINK IN SYSTEMS

- A systems thinking mindset appreciates the complexity and depth of reality itself. It's a higher-order, three-dimensional, dynamic perspective that seeks a broader view on ordinary events.
- The main principle of systems thinking is interconnectedness, i.e. the idea that smaller components arrange themselves in bigger networks or webs. Acknowledging this allows us greater insight and understanding. When we realize that everything within a certain system is interconnected, it allows us to broaden the horizons of our thinking and also tackle problems more

effectively, since we no longer see things in isolation.
- Other principles include synthesis (two things can be combined to create a third, different thing), and emergence (bigger things can arise from the combination of smaller units; the whole is greater than the sum of the parts). Synthesis is an antidote to the reductionism that is a common explanatory toll in our time. When we synthesize, we connect one thing with the other and see how particular links between a few parts affect the whole. Similarly, emergence tells us that small things can aggregate to form one huge thing, an insight that is often overlooked when analyzing specific systems.
- Feedback occurs in systems, either positive (amplifying) or negative (balancing); understanding these cause and effect relationships enhances our understanding and problem-solving capacity.
- We can map/diagram systems according to our needs and perspectives. We can have a system for our workflow, our routine, or for when we tackle specific issues that recur in our lives. By

engaging in systems-based thinking, we make our lives more efficient and easy because we've done the hard part of thinking our actions through. We can also use systems-inspired questions to help us see beyond our limited perspectives.

CHAPTER 6. HOW TO THINK WITH INDUCTION AND DEDUCTION

- Two fundamental paths to arriving at an argument's conclusion include inductive and deductive reasoning. These are also known as merely probable and airtight forms of reasoning based on how valid the conclusions derived from them are.
- Deductive reasoning uses a general principle (such as a theory or known fact) to say something about a specific observation, whereas induction works the other way, trying to establish a general conclusion that can explain the specific observations or given premises.
- Arguments possess both validity and soundness—validity is concerned with the internal logic of an argument, but an argument is only sound if the argument

is logical *and* the premises are true. Thus, an argument can be formally valid, i.e. structured in a valid form, but that doesn't mean it is sound or that it actually holds true. For that, we need to assess the truth value of the premises.

- We can use inductive reasoning to help us fine-tune our powers of observation and "reverse storytelling" to construct probable causes from observations. Inductive arguments always move from specific bits of information which are then used to arrive at a general conclusion. We can use deductive reasoning whenever we are working with known facts or given theories to help us understand new data. It is best employed when we know that the premises of our theories are factually accurate, so as to arrive at true conclusions.

- The fishbone diagram is a good tool to map out inductive arguments. Start by drawing a line through the middle and stating your conclusion at the right end. Along the line, draw diagonal arrows with causes behind that conclusion. Use your deductive skills to further

elaborate on your causes and state the reasons behind them as well.
- Both deductive and indictive reasoning have their place—it's up to us to use them wisely and appropriately, according to the situation at hand.

CPSIA information can be obtained
at www.ICGtesting.com
Printed in the USA
BVHW050351280123
657294BV00003B/50